No More Storms A-Comin'

by
Wales Goebel

with
Janie Buck

No More Storms A-Comin'

Dedicated to Mama

By
Wales Goebel

with
Janie Buck

No More Storms A-Comin'

Dedicated to Mama

by Wales Goebel with Janie Buck

96-83778

For permission to reproduce selections from this book, write to Permissions, Buck Publishing Co. 2409 Vestavia Drive, Birmingham, AL 35216

Graphics and cover design by Katie Cash

Printed in the United States of America

ISBN 0-934530-09-2

Acknowledgements

✥

Books are like people. Each has it own personality. Furthermore, some require a great deal of assistance and support from a team of individuals. I had not been writing long before realizing I needed help. There is so much involved in writing a book that it takes alot of people doing many things.

Looking back I now see this book could not have been written without the skills of Mrs. Janie Buck, or the shared memories of many friends and family.

Mr. and Mrs. Howard Borland, associates of mine for over twenty years, took time to read the manuscript and gave many wonderful suggestions.

Thanks to Betty Jo Bundle Newman, my classmate and good friend, who is supervisor of the Tallapoosa Museum. She and Cliff and Becky Cox, Mary Ann Appling, and Mary Lou Davis read the manuscript several times and added helpful suggestions.

Jean, my wife, deserves special credit. She listened over and over to these chapters as I wrote and re-wrote them.

Enduring thanks to Miss Jan Bearden, my faithful secretary for many, many years. With all the other responsibilities I place on her, she graciously typed, re-typed and corrected this manuscript. Without her, there would be no book.

What's the purpose of the book? That you will see the magnificence of the Lord Jesus Christ!

Contents

1
Bootlegging

I n 1944, the Allies were fighting up the boot of Italy, and the Tallapoosa families whose sons were in the service strongly suspected something big was about to happen. The invasion of France would come off any day.

It galled me that a 15-year old couldn't join up. When I got my driver's permit, Mr. Bentley asked me to drive one of his taxis. I would rather have been in an army tank with the older boys from my county, but since I didn't own a car, driving a taxi was my next choice.

I had learned to drive when I worked at Mr. Evans' grocery store. On the back country roads, out of sight of the police, Joe taught me to drive. Joe worked for Mr. Evans, too, and drove the store truck when we made deliveries.

One reason Mr. Bentley asked me to be a driver was that somewhere on our family tree we were kin. The other reason was that there were practically no men left in town. I didn't care why he asked. Taxis were doing a big business during the war because automobiles were scarce and gasoline was rationed. I was anxious to join the elite fraternity of taxi drivers and jumped at the opportunity without consulting Mama or anybody.

I loved cars and became the hardest-working taxi driver in Tallapoosa, Georgia. Tallapoosa is halfway between Birmingham and Atlanta. Soldiers from Fort McClellan in Anniston, Alabama, and Fort McPherson, near Atlanta, took over our town on Fridays and Saturdays. They came looking for the best Tallapoosa had to offer, and I was there to serve them.

Some of our girls also learned to serve them. They wouldn't turn a trick with a G.I. just for his money. They were patriotic and always said, "It will keep the boys from missing home so much."

I knew some of the girls personally, and they were not what you'd call streetwalkers. Being naive, I really believed some of them saw this as a way of helping the war effort.

One of those girls, Sarah, picked me for her personal driver. She was a pretty girl, no Miss Georgia, but I thought she was too nice to mess around with soldiers. She allowed no one but me to handle her "business." Sarah would stare at me with her big doe eyes and say, "Wales, you are the only one I can trust in my part of the war effort."

Sarah would call for my taxi at 9:00 p.m. and ask me to pick her up at Tupper's Dry Goods Store. She always dressed in her best and smelled of "Evening in Paris," a ten-cent store perfume. Where and how she made her contacts I never knew. But she would instruct me to drive her to where a young soldier, all dressed up in his uniform, was waiting.

I'd drop them off at a dingy little motel on the outskirts of Bremen, Georgia. I knew to come back in two hours. The round-trip fare to Bremen was $4.00. I never once remember Sarah having all the money. Somehow in the next few days she would bring me what she could.

One week she came, four days late, to pay the rest of my fare. I asked, "Sarah, why don't you ask those men to at least give you enough money to pay the taxi bill?"

She was indignant and her eyes flashed when she said, "Why, Wales, I couldn't charge those soldiers. Look at what they're doing for our country! Some of them will never make it back." She threw her pretty brown hair back off her shoulders with a wave of her hand and said, "These men are fighting and dying for you and for me!"

My zealous enthusiasm earned me more trips and more money than the other drivers. But "more money" driving a taxi was only $25.00 a week.

That's why Smokey, one of our more prominent bootleggers, got my attention when he told me he'd pay me big money to make a few "deliveries." It would be easy to make a few special side trips, and I didn't think it illegal to haul the stuff. Making white whiskey was frowned upon by the sheriff's department, but there seemed no harm in

2

my carrying it to a customer.

Mr. Bentley got word of my moonlighting and came to me in a huff. "Wales! I hear you're using my car to run moonshine."

"No, sir! I'm not running whiskey." It wasn't a big black lie, just a little white one. I wasn't "running" whiskey, but making "special deliveries" to the needy.

"Boy, if you ever take whiskey over the state line, it's a federal offense. The law will put you away. You'll go to the state pen and rot in a cell the rest of your life. That is, if they don't give you the electric chair."

I knew he was bluffing, but I acted very serious and swore I'd never do anything like that.

Soon Smokey gave me an assignment. He told me to take one hundred gallons to Anniston, Alabama. Mr. Bentley's warning made me hesitate. "I don't know if I should take whiskey to Alabama, Smokey. I heard I could get in a heap of trouble carrying it over the state line."

"Who's gonna know, boy? The sheriff's got better things to do than stop every car that comes into Alabama."

He was right. Smokey said he had never had trouble before, so I silenced my conscience. It was going to be a long drive, so I asked Buddy to come along and keep me company. The idea of running whiskey was exciting to him. He was ready for the adventure.

I picked him up late one afternoon and headed down Highway 78 toward Alabama. We were yucking it up pretty good as I told him some of my taxi-driving tales. He was enamored with me, and my stories grew bigger for such an appreciative audience.

"You sure live an exciting life, Wales. I wish I could drive a taxi and do what you do."

"Well," I stretched my arms above my head, steered with my knees like I was kind of bored, and said, "that's just the way my life is. One adventure to the next." I felt so smug. I was one exciting fella, and Buddy was real lucky to ride in the car with me.

The tone of Buddy's voice snapped me back from my self importance. "Wales! Is that the police?"

I nearly swallowed the wad of bubble gum I was smacking on. "Police! Where?"

"Up there in the road!"

Sure enough, up ahead were two black and white Alabama sheriff's and state highway patrolmen's cars blocking the road.

"Oh Lord, Oh, Lord." I turned on Buddy. "Did you tell anybody where you were going?"

He looked panic-stricken. His face turned ashen. "Only a couple of folks. I didn't think you'd care."

"Didn't think I'd care?" I roared. "Dang it! Somebody ratted on us. Who'd you tell?"

Buddy opened his mouth, but all that came out was a croak. He was too scared to talk.

The State highway patrol and the sheriff, who were standing in the middle of the road, waved me to stop. I wasn't sure what to do, but I wasn't going to stop. I could now clearly hear Mr. Bentley's warning repeating over and over in my mind. "Don't run whiskey across the state line. They'll put you away! You'll go to the state pen, maybe the electric chair. Don't cross the state line." My eyes darted from the black and white cars ahead into the back seat where my cargo lay. "Put you away forever. Forever..." pounded my brain.

When you start to panic, I guess the gears in your mind automatically downshift into neutral. Mine did, because what else would cause me to speed up and take to the shoulder of the road and maneuver around the roadblock?

"What're you doing?" Buddy found his voice which was now a few octaves higher than usual. At least he was uttering intelligible words.

My mind had temporarily gone out of service. Now I was the one who let out a croak. I could see in my rear-view mirror those lawmen didn't really appreciate my not stopping. The whistle of a bullet over the car roof was my next clue they weren't too happy.

My tires squealed and blue smoke of burning rubber poured out from under the taxi as I slammed on the brakes. I yanked the steering wheel hard and turned onto the first dirt road I saw. It was full of potholes.

Bootlegging

Our heads bashed into the roof as the shocks were put to a full test.

My shirt was immediately drenched with sweat. It coursed down my brow into my eyes. I had to keep wiping it away so I could see where to go in the twilight.

"Crack, crack, crack." More shots from the police. They sounded like fire crackers exploding around us.

"Stop! Stop! You're going to get us killed!" Buddy was screaming at me and reaching for the steering wheel. I punched him as hard as I could to get him away from the wheel. Suddenly, a bullet grazed my side mirror. Buddy looked over his shoulder and shrieked, "They're gaining on us!"

I wanted to cry, but there was nothing I could do. I was about to die and get Buddy killed. It was either be shot or go to the electric chair.

We skidded around the next corner. I thought the car would flip. Amazingly it didn't, and Buddy's pleas finally shifted my mind out of neutral. I stopped just as abruptly as I had speeded up.

The police cars almost rear-ended us. They were not expecting me to slam on my brakes in the middle of their high-speed chase. I've never seen men move as fast as those lawmen. They jumped out of the black and whites and jerked me out of the driver's seat before the dust stopped swirling around the cars.

Slam! The sheriff hurled me onto the hood of my car. My face burned on the metal from the overworked engine. I heard Buddy explaining that he was only along for the ride and had no part in whiskey running. I tried to turn my face to look at him. "Oof!" A billy club was thrust into the back of my neck to hold me down. The sheriff, deputies, and state patrolmen screamed at us. I heard the car doors and trunk being ripped open. A club against my neck cut off my wind. I was choking. I pounded on the hood with my fist, trying to call out. The pressure only increased.

"Hold still, boy!" the patrolman hissed with an emphasis on "still" as he shoved his club harder into my neck. I groaned. My ears rang and everything went blurry. Just as I was about to pass out, relief was granted. The sheriff jerked me backwards by my collar. I gasped for air and took in gulps like I had been drowning. My arms were wrenched behind my back. The handcuffs closed around my wrists and bit into my flesh. I stumbled as strong arms shoved me toward the wailing siren on the patrol cars.

"Shut that blasted thing off," the sheriff bellowed.

I was pushed into the back seat of the squad car with my hands cuffed behind me. Why, why, why had I not heeded Mr. Bentley's warning? What was I going to tell Mama? I leaned my head against the window and watched as Buddy, uncuffed and scared, was put into the other police car. I heard the sheriff tell the other officer to drive him back to Tallapoosa.

Not a word was said during the long ride into town. The back of the sheriff's neck was red as a beet. His veins protruded from his temples. He ground his teeth all the way back to Anniston, Alabama.

As we pulled in front of the police station, a woman came out of the building and peered in at me. The sheriff got out, slamming the door behind him. I heard him and the woman exchange some heated words. I knew their conversation was aimed at me because he kept gesturing toward the car.

Next he opened my door, grabbed my arm, and pulled me out.

"He's just a boy," the woman said. "For heavens sake, don't put him upstairs with all the older men and drunks."

He marched me past her and up the steps of the jail house. I didn't look into her eyes, but just dropped my head on my chest. Once inside I kept my eyes on the floor as he marched me to where they usually kept women prisoners.

I have never forgotten the sound of the cold metal bars of the jail door closing behind me. Even now, years later, the memory brings shivers. It rang with a tone of "they'll put you away forever!"

The sheriff's footsteps echoed through the empty hall as he left. He shut an outer door and left me all alone. Alone. I never felt so lonely in all my life. I fell to my knees beside the bunk and cried.

Time runs strange when you're alone in a jail cell. Five minutes can seem like an hour, so I'm not sure how long I was in there before I heard the outer door open. The footsteps in the hall sounded lighter than the sheriff's.

I stood up and blinked twice to make sure it was really the woman who had been outside when we drove up. She unlocked the cell door and inserted a key into the handcuffs to free my hands. She then told me to sit down. "I'm the sheriff's wife," she explained as my face showed my bewilderment. "Where are you from, son?"

"Tallapoosa, ma'am," I answered, trying to sound respectful.

"Whose car were you driving, honey?"

I asked, "Do you know Mr. Bentley?"

"Why, yes I do."

She looked at me a few moments as if thinking about what to do, nodded her head, and got up to leave. I was sad to see her go and hated hearing that clang of the jail door again. I leaned back against the cold cement wall. I thought, Mr. Bentley was right. It was just a matter of time until they hauled me off to the state pen.

Time passed slowly. A few hours later, I heard the door open again and knew by the footsteps it was the sheriff.

He stood in front of the cell door and stared at me for a while. He finally put the key into the lock, opened the door, and stated, "You're free to go."

I couldn't believe what he was saying. I just sat there stunned. Slowly I stood to my feet and walked out tentatively, afraid it was a joke and that he'd slam the door in my face.

"Go on, boy! GO!"

When I walked out the front door, my eyes fell on none other than Mr. Bentley. I'd never been subject to such a tongue-lashing as I got from him. It was almost as bad as being pinned by the sheriff's billy club. His face was purple, little blue veins popped out on his temples, and flecks of spit came shooting from his lips after every other word. I'd never seen anyone but my Dad so angry. Dad would have been beating me, but Mr. Bentley's words had the same effect.

"Yes sir, yes sir, no sir, never again," I swore.

"If you do, I'll let you rot in jail, and you'll never drive for me again."

I had never been so relieved in all my life. He need not worry about my ever doing that again. The drive back to Tallapoosa was a ride to freedom.

I was never so content just to drive a taxi again. Never would money cloud my judgment as it did this time. No amount of money was worth repeating my Alabama jail experience.

Yet, somehow the resolve of a 15-year-old didn't amount to too much. I didn't learn until years later that New Year's resolutions and determined resolves to reform failed every time without the Lord's power working within me. But that's another story.

2
Mama Won't Be Hurt

At 17, I was a very responsible citizen of Tallapoosa. The local town folks would wave and call, "Hello, Wales!" as I passed by in my taxi. I returned their waves, pleased with myself. It had been two years since my run-in with the Alabama sheriff, and I had kept away from the bootleggers. No more "deliveries" for me.

One hot summer afternoon, Wade, an older school friend and also a driver for Mr. Bentley, came sauntering over to my taxi.

"Hi ya', Wales," he said, leaning in my passenger window. "How's business?"

I knew he was up to something because he was grinning like a butcher's dog. He opened the door and climbed in. The springs in the seat gave a moan under his weight, and the door creaked when he slammed it.

"Sounds like your taxi's complainin' a little," he chuckled like it was a great joke.

"What do you want, Wade? Did you come over just to harass me about my car?"

Wade draped his long arm across the back of the seat and asked me for a cigarette. He lit up and took a deep drag before he answered. "Wales, I've got a business proposition to make you." He spoke with a twinkle in his eye like "just wait till you hear this."

He had piqued my curiosity, so I decided to let him speak his piece. "How's that?"

"Next week a construction crew is coming into Tallapoosa to put in a new gas line." He was having a hard time containing his excitement and trying to play it cool at the same time. "Now, if we are smart, we can make a wad of money."

Dollar signs flashed across my mind. He had my attention, but I wasn't sure we would earn much more driving the gas-line men to the local taverns.

"So?" I challenged.

"These men are a rowdy bunch and love our special made," he lowered his voice to a whisper, "Georgia whiskey."

"Wade, you're asking me to be a bootlegger?" It was good the police chief wasn't standing on the corner for he would have heard me. Wade waved me to hold it down, but I had my dander up.

"You act like it's as easy as taking them to Baby Hat's Cafe for chili. You don't know what it's like to hear the jail cell door close on you." I shuddered with the memory. "It's just not a smart thing to do. There's no way I'd ever run whiskey. No way. Never!"

Wade shrugged, then threw in the baited hook. "That's too bad, Wales. You could make $50 a day." He made like he was about to get out of the car.

That was more money than I had ever seen. I suddenly forgot all about that jail cell and without a second thought took the bait.

Grabbing his arm, I asked, "Are you sure?"

He had already figured the ins and outs and excitedly related his plan to me. "The taxis will be our legitimate business, and we can sell the whiskey from them."

Listening to him ramble on with his plans, I squirmed in my seat when I thought of Mama. If I got caught, it would kill her. Mama had tried so hard to raise her boys to be respectable, and I didn't want to let her down. I didn't think again about jail. The prospects of big-time money were too strong for even Mama's hurt to matter. Before I knew it ,we were heading down a dusty road to Smokey Johnson's home.

Smokey was known for making good whiskey. If I was going to sell it, I wanted to make sure my customers didn't go blind. This could happen from poorly made moonshine.

Smokey leaned his shotgun by the rusty screen door on his sagging front porch and ambled out to my taxi. He deftly shifted the sweet-gum twig to the corner of his mouth and quoted his price, $3 a gallon.

We decided to start with three gallons. That was all the money we had between us. On our way back to town, we talked about what we'd do with all the profits. We were headed for untold riches.

I pulled up to our taxi stand. It was next to the old boarding house Wade's mother ran. "Mother would kill us if she knew what we were up to, but there is a bathroom on the second floor that's not rented. It'll make a good place to divide the whiskey," Wade said. We poured the moonshine into a #2 wash tub and dipped half-pint bottles in. I counted the bottles while Wade poured up the last drops of the potent liquid. It made me nearly drunk just smelling the stuff. We had 48 half pints. Why we could sell these for $1.25 a bottle which would land us a $57.00 profit!

It didn't take long for word to get around that we were selling. People started calling for a delivery. Some folks would just climb in the taxi, buy a couple of bottles, and then hop out. Men would wave us down and buy it on the streets.

Wade and I became Al Capone and Bugsy Moran of Tallapoosa. Business was really good. Every day, it got better.

Wade and I usually went together when we made a pickup at Smokey's. We did this so that if anything happened, we would face the music together. But one day, I went alone. I drove out in the country toward Smokey's and passed the pipeline men who were digging a ditch down the middle of the road. I had to slow down to get past their dirt and machinery. They didn't seem to mind the dust my car made because they knew I would have plenty of white whiskey ready for them when they got off work. I leaned out the window and shouted, "I'll see you fellas later."

I wanted to pick up six gallons, but others had made a run on Smokey. He had only three gallons left. This turned out to be good luck.

As I headed back to town, a sheriff's car was blocking the road where the gas-line ditch started. I stopped, and my heart almost stopped, too. Drops of sweat trickled down my brow as I considered my options. I slammed my Ford in reverse and backed up fast. A rooster tail of gravel flung up from the tires and rattled the fenders like hail on a tin roof.

Glancing up the road, all I could see was the black and white police car. The sheriff had swung around and was closing the gap between us. My hand was shaking as I rounded a corner. I reached into the back seat and grabbed the sack of whiskey. The wail of the siren screamed, but the sheriff's car was out of sight. I slung the sack as hard as I could across the ditch into high weeds.

I kept backing till I came to the end of the ditch and pulled to one side to wait. The police were 30 seconds behind me. This gave me just enough time to get out of the Ford. I sat on the running board looking innocent as an egg-sucking dog.

The police car skidded sideways to avoid my taxi, and a cloud of dust nearly choked me. The sheriff's face was a picture of "I gotcha!" He slammed the door of the squad car and walked slowly toward me with his hand on his holster. He pushed me out of the way and, speaking through gritted teeth, ordered his grinning deputies to search the car.

The sheriff stood staring in my face the whole time as if to force a confession. When they found nothing, one deputy walked up the road to look for the evidence. It didn't take him long to discover my recently abandoned whiskey.

The smell of chewing tobacco on the sheriff's breath was withering as he stood toe to toe with me and shouted for an explanation. I feigned ignorance. That sack didn't have my name on it.

I tried not to let my face betray disappointment as the deputy poured my profits on the ground. I shifted from one foot to the other watching the whiskey turn the dust to mud.

The sheriff wanted to hang me from the nearest tree but sent me on with an "I'll get you next time" expression that only a Georgia sheriff can give when beaten.

It was only a couple of weeks later when Wilson got in my car at the taxi stand. He wasn't smiling. "What's the matter, Wilson?"

"Wales, the law is going to send you to the pen."

Shivers ran up and down my back. "How do you know?" I asked, not sure I believed him.

He told me he had heard a deputy say they were on my tail. It was just a matter of time till they'd lock me away. I thanked him and sat there for about an hour after he left, considering if the cash was worth it.

Wade drove up behind me and strolled over to my taxi. He leaned into my open window. "I'm quitting, Wade." I had made up my mind. (I've often wondered if God sent Wilson to protect me from real serious troubles.)

He stood straight up in startled unbelief. I recounted my conversation with Wilson. "Aw, Wales, he's just trying to scare you off because he's selling and wants your business" Then he tried to pull his ace again, "Besides what about all the money you're making? We still have several gallons to get rid of."

I leaned out the window and grabbed his shirt sleeve to try to make him understand. "Wade, it's yours. All of it. You know, if Wilson is right and I get caught, it would kill Mama. As for myself, I wouldn't care, but I just can't hurt Mama."

"Taxi!" a woman called from across the street at Mr. Evans' grocery store. I let Wade's shirt go. He gave me a mock salute as I pulled around to pick up my customer.

The next night, my taxi door creaked open. I saw the glow of a hand-rolled cigarette balanced on the lower lip of an old black man. "Half a pint," he mumbled without any introduction.

"Fresh out, but I can take you where the moon's always shining."

I saw the glow of the cigarette burn bright orange as he took a deep drag. He climbed in the back seat and said, "Drive on."

When we arrived at Mrs. Bell's shot house, she told me she was dry. Her cheap perfume invaded my nostrils as she leaned in close to whisper the sheriff was watching.

The old man looked disgruntled when I returned to the car empty-handed. I ducked back into the driver's seat. "Well, I know of one other place we can try."

Just as I pulled onto the main road, headlights came at me from every direction. The ear-piercing scream of several squad cars told me who was hemming me in. My car was immediately surrounded by all kinds of badges. The sheriff yanked the doors open, pulled me and the black man out, and growled into my face, "We've got you now, boy! There are no weeds to throw your whiskey in this time."

The boys in blue seemed to take pleasure in ripping out my seats and shining their flashlights in every nook and cranny of the trunk. They stripped my car, even removing the hubcaps which clanged loudly as they dropped on the pavement.

I stood in the middle of the road staring beyond the end of the sheriff's gun pointing at me like I would try to escape. My mouth felt dry as the dusty Georgia roads, and my heart pounded as I stood watching the steam rise up in front of the head-lights. The deputies looked like ghostly shadows moving through the darkness searching for something that wasn't there.

I tried to act calm, because I was really clean this time. But the shock of realizing Wilson was right and the knowledge of my close call was enough to make me tremble. I shook myself trying to gain composure. The sheriff shoved his gun at me. "Don't even think about running," he warned.

"We can't find anything, sheriff," came the long-awaited reply of the deputy.

"Look some more," said the sheriff. He didn't want to be wrong a second time.

"We've turned the car inside out."

That was true. I looked around and saw the ground was strewn with every loose piece they could pull out of my car.

The sheriff glared at me and reholstered his gun. He didn't say a word. He just turned on his heels and got into his squad car. The other deputies took that as a sign and climbed into their cars. All drove off leaving me and the black man alone with my car all torn down.

I sat on the running board and put my head in my hands. The crickets and night creatures resumed their songs as if they also had been holding their breath. My shoulders began to shake and I kind of snorted. Then I burst out laughing, but tears were running down my cheeks.

I sat there just half laughing and half crying.

The black man started backing up. "Boy," he said, "you've done lost yore mind." He had been afraid he was going to get taken off to jail. There wasn't a thing to laugh about.

I slapped the running board to get him to sit down beside me. He reluctantly took a seat. I put my hand on his shoulder and said, "I'll let you in on my joke. I just quit selling yesterday!"

I couldn't seem to hold it back and let my laughter ring out into the dark night. The man just kind of grinned and shook his head.

One thing for sure, Mama wouldn't be hurt. For that I was relieved beyond words.

.

3
There's A Storm A-Comin'

Mama was my security. I can't remember Dad ever saying he loved me or speaking a kind word. Because Mama loved me, I tried hard to please her. My earliest memory of her was when I was only six.

I can still see her standing on the back porch watching the black clouds churning in the sky. The wind bent the trees and blew her dress and apron straight out from her stout body. Mama's hands and face were weatherworn and wrinkled for a young woman. Living with a hard man and the Depression made it necessary for her to take in washing. She was strong and not afraid of hard work. She washed clothes for us, and the neighbors, in tubs sitting on benches by the well. Big black iron wash pots heated water and boiled the dirty clothes clean. To this day, I still associate clean clothes with burning firewood.

Mama leaned against the wind looking out over the woods and pasture behind our house. She watched over her boys like a hawk circling a chicken yard. When she didn't see her two little boys, she hollered, "Wales! You boys get into the house right now! There's a storm a-comin'."

Some folks say when Mama hollered for us you could hear her all over the county. Seaborn and I reluctantly left our game of cowboys and Indians and raced out of the woods and followed Mama into the kitchen. The wind slammed the screen door behind us. We took our places on the smooth worn benches and slouched down with our elbows on the oilcloth- covered table to watch Mama make us cocoa and toast. She smiled at five-year-old Seaborn who cowered like a scared rabbit during thunderstorms.

The wind raised the tin off the roof and slammed it down onto the rafters. I would look up at the ceiling to make sure it wasn't going to fly away to the land of Oz. The sheet lightning and thunder in the hot summer Georgia sky was enough to scare the clothes off a scarecrow. Rain poured off the roof and beat against the bare wooden boards covering our home. As long as it didn't come in, I felt safe. Not that I was brave, but Mama's presence consoled me.

Southern summer storms never last too long. Soon the roar of rain beating the tin turned into a soft pitter patter, and the thunder rumbled off toward Atlanta. When Mama thought it was safe, we headed out of our small weathered refuge and ventured back out into the lush green woods to resume our games. She always warned us to watch where we stepped. Barefoot boys might cut their feet on pieces of tin that may have blown off somebody's house or barn or step on a roofing nail. Most children in Tallapoosa went barefoot all summer. The wet grass felt good under foot. The water dripping off the leaves made everything lush and beautiful. I shook a low tree branch and showered water onto Seaborn's head.

"Cut it out, Wales."

"Make me!" I retorted.

That started a mad wrestling match. Dirt and wet leaves clung to our clothes and hair as we struggled. I had the advantage since I was older and bigger and dominated the match. When I heard the screen door slam, I froze. Daddy was home early. He left the grocery store for my half brother Robert to close up for the night.

Dad wasn't from Georgia. He and his first wife and five sons had moved to Tallapoosa from Chicago because of one son's asthma. The doctor thought the warmer weather would be better for him.

Dad was a shrewd businessman and had prospered in the South. He had first grown grapes on a hundred acres and made excellent wine. Prohibition stopped the sale of all liquors. It was around that time that his wife died.

When his wine business went sour, he built a large hotel. Tallapoosa was the perfect place for salesmen to stop for the night because it was halfway between Atlanta and Birmingham. Daddy was an accomplished

musician and played the piano in the hotel parlor during dinner hour.
He must have been something back then, driving a nice car, wearing
fancy clothes, and owning that beautiful new hotel. I guess that's why
Mama fell in love with him. He was older and must have seemed very
distinguished. Mama was only 16 when they married. They lived in the
hotel, and I was born there.

When the Depression hit and closed the banks, Daddy lost all his
money. The hotel was sold. It was quite a change for Mama to move
three blocks away into the little house where I grew up.

I tried to stay out of Daddy's way because he had a violent temper.
Maybe it was the hardship he had been through, but I can't remember
him ever showing any love for Mama or my five half brothers and two
real brothers.

Seaborn and I quit our wrestling and listened when we heard him
yelling at Mama. We climbed up in our fort in the trees to escape
harm's way. I reached up and felt the back of my head remembering
how once his knuckles struck me after I had asked him for a dime.
Seaborn and I had wanted to go to the picture show. In those days we
could see an "Our Gang" comedy, a "Flash Gordon" serial, and then a
"Buck Jones" or "Red Ryder" movie for a nickel apiece.

"The money is not available," Dad had said, giving me a look that
let me know he wasn't pleased with me. When I turned to leave, a blow
from his large fist struck me on the back of the head. I lay sprawled on
the floor and looked up at him, bewildered. His expression frightened
me more than the warning growled through gritted teeth, "Don't ever
ask me for picture-show money again!"

I didn't resent him for not giving money to me. I knew times were
hard for everyone during the Great Depression.

There was one prosperous family I knew in Tallapoosa. At least the
Calhouns seemed that way in my eyes. They had real shiny linoleum on
their floors. We had only bare wood that Mama scrubbed with a corn
shuck brush. The Calhoun boys wore clothes from the Sears and
Roebuck catalog instead of homemade shirts like the other kids in
town. I told Mama we could have nice things, too, if she would sell

whiskey out our back door like Mrs. Calhoun did. Mama's response to my reasoning was, "I may be poor, but I'm proud."

My pleasures were simple in those days. We made our own toys. A stick made a top-notch gun, the trees were our forts, and the woods our playground. Those days seemed so carefree and simple. The Depression wasn't as painful for a child of six as it was to adults. Daddy was lucky. He still had a home and a business.

Everyone had some kind of storm in their life back then. In the distance there were "storms a-comin'" for me. I couldn't see them at first, but they came in full force and beat me worse than any whipping Daddy ever gave me. Lots of well-intentioned people like Mr. Bentley tried to warn me. Mama tried to hold them back, but my storms were too big, even for her. When I was running from the sheriff, I wished Mama could save me like when she rescued me from a bully.

It seemed I couldn't stay out of fights, even when I was just playing marbles!

After school one day, I went over to play marbles with James. He drew a circle in the dirt with his big toe, marking our game field. We both put ten marbles in the center. Then we examined each other's "taw." A "taw" was the main marble we shot with. Some boys used "steelies," but they would knock the marbles a mile and break them.

Mr. Kilgore's five-and-ten-cent store sold marbles for a nickel a bag. That was a lot of money for me. One bag a summer was my limit. The idea in playing was to win the other boy's marbles. If you were good you'd win enough marbles to play all summer, and I was good. When school started that year, I had over 20 marbles.

My "taw" was red and white. It took precedence over "Useless," my dog, and girls, who were more than useless. It ranked right up there with oatmeal cookies. My "taw" was the last thing I put down at night and the first thing I picked up each morning. I carefully placed it in my pocket before my #2 pencil and my favorite treasure—a "Buck" knife.

James and I pitched a penny to a line to see who shot first. I won. It was an advantage to shoot first, like in shooting pool, as I would later learn. The one who broke got to scatter the marbles just like in billiards. I rubbed my "taw" between my palms and said a few magic words. Carefully I placed my fist on the ground outside the ring. My thumb pushed the "taw" forward and it shot out like a cannon ball. Marbles flew everywhere.

Every time I shot, James jeered and beat the ground with his fist. His attempted distractions didn't bother me a bit. I soon cleared the ring and won all his marbles.

He fumed and wanted revenge and challenged me to another game. He was having a good summer, too, and still had ten marbles. This time James won the break. He shot three marbles out of the ring before missing. My turn. I did the same thing as before and cleared the circle. The way my "taw" was working, I could have beaten the national marble-shooting champion.

James was hopping mad. He picked up his empty marble bag and stalked off. "I'll get even with you, Wales!" he shouted over his shoulder.

I thought he meant in marbles. I wasn't concerned because I had my winning taw.

Whistling a tune we learned in school, I called, "Come on, Useless." My old red-bone hound jumped up from the sand bed, wagging his tail. "Let's go home, boy." I scratched his bony head.

James called my name. I turned around to see him running full blast towards me. I started to run too. Now I knew what he meant by "get even."

I jumped a fence and ran through the pasture with James gaining on me. Mama was washing clothes by the well. When I reached her, I thought I was safe.

She asked, "Wales, are you running from that boy?"

"Yes, ma'am," I said catching my breath and taking refuge behind her skirt.

"You get yourself right out there where he is! If you don't, I'll whip you harder than any ten boys," she said.

I looked at James, then at Mama's stern face. I decided it would be

James. Reluctantly, I walked back out to the pasture. He was on me like a cat on a mouse.

My little brother had followed me and stood there watching. James was stronger than I and sat on top of me and kept hitting me in the face. I begged my brother for help, but he was too scared to move.

James was known not to take captives. He might have killed me, but I heard a loud crack and he fell over in the grass. He rolled over three times, jumped up, looked at Mama, and ran like a scared rabbit. I looked up into Mama's wonderful face.

"You all right, son?" Mama asked, still holding the battling paddle she used to beat dirt out of overalls.

"Yes, ma'am." I gladly took her hand and she pulled me to my feet.

"Come on home now, and I'll wash your cuts."

"Can we use mercurochrome on them?" I asked, knowing it wouldn't burn like iodine.

"No, things that don't hurt are not always the most helpful."

I didn't understand what she meant, but as I grew older, I discovered that if something hurt bad enough, I quit doing it. But peace was a long way off for I had only begun to hurt.

All my young life was filled with storms. It took years before the wind quit blowing and peace came.

4
Hobos

Whites and blacks lived peaceably together in the South during the thirties. That is all except the Ku Klux Klan, and they kept their faces covered. Only a few whites went along with the Klan. Fear kept the whites, who did object, from speaking out against Klansmen. We never knew if the sheriff, the chief of police, or our neighbor belonged to it.

When we heard a whipping had taken place, Mama would say, "The Klan is nothing but white trash. Every last one of them ought to be put in a hole and covered with dirt." I thought Mama would cover the hole if someone dug it.

Some black boys were my good friends, and one black man helped point the way out of my storms. Two of the biggest black men in the South unknowingly inspired me.

It happened one summer when I was six. I was sitting on the back porch steps watching little red ants hurrying in and out of their ant bed. To me they were a trained battalion of misery. I hated them. When I accidentally stepped on their bed, they marched undetected up my leg until they covered the whole thing. At their drill master's command, the little devils commenced stinging simultaneously. That was a declaration of war, so I poked their bed with a long stick and danced around the ruined ant bed giving Indian war whoops and lifting my stick to the sky like it was a bow and arrow.

In the midst of my battle, a dark shadow come over me and the ants. Four of the biggest brogans I'd ever seen stood at the end of the shadow. The shoes were totally worn out with the soles nearly gone. The old laces were tied in several knots. My eyes climbed up the legs to the worn-out knees of dirty overalls and up and up until I fell back upon my ant battlefield. The midday sun was eclipsed by the heads of two giant black men standing before me. They looked nine feet tall.

Suddenly I felt the stings of retaliation from my forgotten war. I jumped up hollering and slapping my arms and legs and did a better war dance than before. One of the giants squatted down and with two swipes of his huge hand brushed the ants off. I was so grateful I didn't mind them laughing. With a broad grin one of them drawled, "Anybody home beside you?"

I wasn't one bit afraid, just astonished at their size.

"Yes, sir," I responded, still scratching the red welts forming on my arms and legs. "Mama's inside."

"Reckon we could speak to her?" the other one requested.

"I guess so."

I heard the old screen door creak on its rusty hinges behind me. We all looked up to see Mama standing on the weathered porch wiping her hands on her apron. She looked compassionately at the black men and asked, "You boys looking for something to eat?"

"Yes, ma'am," they looked down, removed their straw hats and held them behind their backs. Looking up, one added, "But we don't want food for nothing. We're willing to do chores for whatever you give us."

"Well, you sit right there on the steps and I'll go fix a plate. You look too hungry for me to get any work out of you first." She smiled and disappeared through the screen door.

"Yes, ma'am. We's hungry," they called after her.

Fascinated I sat next to them. I was at once aware of their strong body odor. I thought, "If Mama gets a whiff of them, she'll give them a bar of Octagon soap, make them draw some well water, get in her wash tub, and bathe."

Their smell didn't bother me any. I asked if they ever hunted possum. They smiled and their eyes got big and bright.

"Yes, sir, boy, I've sure done a mess of possum hunting," one said. "The best meat in the world comes from the possum. It's much better than rabbit or frog legs. Possum meat and a big bowl of greens is hard to beat. Don't reckon your mama has any."

"No, sir," I shook my head. "Mama don't like dead things. She likes to cook things that grow. She makes dandy hoecakes. Her eggs with cut-up potatoes and toast cooked in her oven, along with hot chocolate, is the best in all the world."

Mama came out with bowls full of greens, potatoes, slaw, cornbread and sorghum syrup, plenty of buttermilk, and an onion.

"When you boys finish," she said, "I got a job for you before you get your dessert." Her eyes scanned the yard in search of chores she needed tending to.

They ate like they were starving.

"You got a good Mama, boy," one man said, as he wiped his mouth on his sleeve.

"Yes, sir," I said, feeling a little proud. "Where's your mama?"

"Oh, she's a long way away," he answered with a far-off look in his eyes.

"Why did you leave her?"

"Looking for work," he answered. "There's not much work in my hometown because of this Depression."

"Well, Mama will let you cut kindling."

"That's mighty kind of her," he smiled at me.

"Yes, sir, that's mighty good eatin'," the other joined in. "The Lord has blessed you with a good Mama."

"You gonna see your mama soon?" I asked.

"I don't know," he kicked the dirt at the bottom of the steps where we sat. "Wish I could."

"Can your mama cook as good as Mama?"

"Well, now, I don't know," he answered and looked off down the road. "When I eat at my Mama's table, I say she can't be beat. But when I eat your Mama's vittles, I almost swear they are the best I ever put in my mouth." He gave me a snaggle-toothed grin.

"Wait till you eat her banana pudding." Just thinking about it made me hungry.

"Lordy, Lordy, we'd better get on them slabs so we can get to that pudding," he said as he reached out to help his friend up. They walked slowly over to the wood pile. I was so happy 'cause I wouldn't have to chop wood for a while.

I sat on the well curb and watched them cut the slabs Daddy had gotten from the lumber yard. Never had I seen muscles as big as theirs except in pictures of Charles Atlas. I had cut his picture out of a magazine and kept it in my dresser drawer. Mr. Atlas had been a weak and skinny kid and others picked on him. After he began an exercise program to develop his body, he was known as Mr. America. One day, when I got some money, I wanted to order his body-building kit so I could have muscles like his.

I asked the black men if they had taken a Charles Atlas course.

"Don't believe I know him. What does he do?"

"He's big like you," I said.

"Wales, come and get this water," Mama called. She held out two half-gallon fruit jars full of cold well water. "Give it to those men."

I held a jar under each arm and walked to the wood pile. "Ya'll want some water?"

"Sure do," they said and dropped their axes.

They turned the jars up and drank it all, losing only a few drops that ran out the sides of their mouths.

"Want some more?" I asked.

"Naw, not now," they said. "That was just fine."

I'd never seen anyone cut wood so fast. They split a whole slab in one lick and cut it up to stove size in no time. Sure was going to make my winter chores easier. It was up to me and my brother, Seaborn, to get the coal, kindling, and wood for Mama's kitchen stove and our fireplace. We didn't mind bringing in wood because Mama's stove had to be hot before she could cook.

I had an idea and ran into the kitchen. "Mama, can those two men live with us?"

"I don't know about that," she said. "Where would they sleep?"

"We could make a pallet in the front room."

"Why would you want them to stay with us?" she asked.

"Mama, they cut slabs faster than the saw at the planer mill. And they could teach me their course."

"What course?" she asked.

"The one they took from Mr. Atlas to get big muscles," I answered.

"Those boys didn't get muscles from taking a course," she said.

"Well, how did they get them, Mama?"

"By hard work. If you want big muscles, you have to work hard. You have to cut a lot of slabs if you want to look like those men."

I raised my arm, pulled up my sleeve. "Have I got big muscles, Mama?"

"For a six-year-old, you have fine muscles," she said.

I walked back out to the wood pile. "What do y'all do for a living?"

"We's hobos," they said.

"Hobo? What's a hobo?"

"We's folks who can't find steady work, so we go from town to town and do odd jobs," they answered.

"Do you find many jobs?" I asked.

"No, sir," one said, as his ax slammed into a slab. "Sometimes we go for days before folks give us work. And when hobos don't work, they don't eat."

"You don't eat for days?" I asked, unbelieving.

"Sure don't," they said. "Sometimes not for days. Your Mama is the first one to give us a job since we jumped off the train yesterday."

"You ride the train?"

"Yes, sir, all hobos do."

"I never have rode a train in all my life." I was more fascinated with them now. "But I sure do want to. I have an uncle who lives in Birmingham, and he rides free. Next summer he's coming to get me and we'll ride the No. 7 from Tallapoosa to Birmingham. You ever been to Birmingham?"

"No, but we're headin' that way," they answered. "Reckon your Mama would mind putting some more water in these jars? We's mighty thirsty."

I grabbed the jars and ran into the house.

"Mama, they need you to fill these again," I said.

"Go draw a bucket of water from the well," she said.

I brought the water in. Mama knocked a couple of chunks from the ice block in the ice box. She put them in the jars and filled them with water.

Again I tucked the jars under my arms and went back to the wood-pile. They thanked me, turned up the jars, and again didn't stop drinking till the jars were empty. This time no water ran down the sides of their mouths. They took the ice, rubbed it all over their faces, and handed me the empty jars.

"I wish ya'll didn't have to go," I said. "If you stay, I'll get my half-brother, Robert, and his friend, Mr. Joe, who is black like you, and we could go possum huntin'."

"That's nice of you," one said. "But we hear there is steady work at the steel mills in Birmingham."

"When you get to Birmingham, go see my Uncle Andy. He'll get you work on the railroad. But you might not want to work for him since you ride free already."

"Yes, sir, we sure do. We ride free."

When they finished cutting and stacking the wood, they told Mama thanks for the work and vittles. "Your boy sure kept the water coming."

Mama gave each of them a dime and a sandwich in a brown paper sack. She whispered something in one of their ears.

They turned to walk toward the railroad. Then the one Mama had whispered to turned and came back. He looked down and said, "Where did a young boy like you get such big muscles?"

I looked up and stretched my arm out and pumped up my muscle. "You want to feel it?" I asked.

He felt my arm. "I never knew anybody as young as you with such a big muscle," he said.

Mama pulled me close to her. We watched them walk down the dirt road and out of sight.

"Mama, you think I got a big muscle?" I asked, looking up into her soft eyes.

"Biggest I ever seen on a six-year-old," she said.

5
My Best Christmas

Money got so scarce we had to have the current cut off in our little unpainted house. Our electric bill was $4 a month, but that was more than we could afford. For light, we used kerosene lamps. We all sat around the kitchen table with the lamp in the middle. The soft glow of the lamp didn't go far, but as a child, I thought it was magical.

The damp cold of the Georgia winter cut through our un-insulated house. Our only heat was the fireplace in the front room and Mama's stove in the kitchen. Sitting around the fireplace, my front side got hot and my backside froze. The lamp on the table by Daddy's chair and the fire supplied enough light for us boys to play with our homemade toys.

Seaborn and I slept in the loft under the tin roof. We toasted ourselves by the stove before racing up the steps and jumping between the icy sheets. The weight of the quilts Mama piled on our bed cuddled us deep in the feather mattress. Soon our body's heat warmed the bed so we could drift off to sleep.

I always carried the lamp upstairs when Seaborn and I went to bed. Mama warned me every night to blow out the flame before setting the lamp down. Our house was made of heart pine. It would burn like kindling. The fear of setting our house on fire made my hands sweat.

A few nights before Christmas, Mama asked Seaborn and me to sit down at the table before we made our climb upstairs. She took our hands in hers. A tear rolled down her cheek. "Boys, times are hard right now. Santa Claus is not going to be able to come to our house this year."

I looked at five-year-old Seaborn. His little forlorn face told me this news made him feel the same as me. A spark of hope flickered in my heart. I ventured, "Maybe Santa will have a few leftovers for us."

"No," Mama said, dropping our hands. She turned her back to us. "There won't be anything." Her shoulders sagged and her head went down.

"What if some little boy gets something he don't like? Maybe we could have that," Seaborn said, not convinced we would be overlooked.

"You boys are just dreaming," Mama replied and brushed tears from her cheeks. "Might as well get it into your heads, there will be no Christmas presents this year."

"Not even a box of chocolate-covered cherries?" I asked with desperation. We always had chocolate-covered cherries under the tree. I loved them almost as much as I loved Mama. When I nibbled a hole in the top, I could suck the sweet juice out before crunching into the chocolate and cherry inside.

"I'm afraid not. Maybe next year," Mama said, and kissed our woe-begone faces before we climbed up to bed. It was hard to go to sleep with the burden on our minds of no Santa Claus. We talked a little about such an unheard-of possibility before we fell into a fitful sleep.

My heart was heavy at school the next day. On the way home, I stopped and looked in the window of Lipham's Dry Goods store. I pressed my face on the glass. I could hardly believe my eyes. The window was filled with toys. There were guns, cowboy suits, baseball gloves, footballs, and a bag of the prettiest red marbles I'd ever seen. Surely Santa could find something for me and my brother in all those toys.

I flung open the door and I ran up to the clerk. "Excuse me, will you please tell Santa where my brother and I live. I wanted him to know that no matter what he has left over after visiting the children in Tallapoosa, to please come by our house. We live at 25 Stokes Street." I felt sure the matter was settled.

"Son, I don't know if I'll see him, but if I do, I'll tell him." The clerk was as serious as I.

"Can I see that bag of red marbles?" I asked.

"Sure you can." She reached in the window to get them. I held on to them, turning them over and over in my hands as if they were the finest rubies.

"How much would these cost?" I asked.

"A nickel," she said. "Do you have a nickel?"

"No, ma'am." I held them a little longer before thanking her and handing them back. An idea popped in my head as I skipped all the way home.

I burst in our front door. "Mama, can we have a Christmas tree? If Santa Claus did come and didn't see a tree, he wouldn't know if any children lived here. He might go away," I reasoned.

"Santa Claus is not coming, tree or not. But if you want one, you can go cut one down," she said.

I hardly took time to eat the oatmeal cookies and drink the glass of milk Mama had set on the table for me. There was still a chance Santa might visit. Before Seaborn and I dashed out the door, Mama said, "Don't cut a big one. 'Bout like we had last year."

"Yes, ma'am."

I ran to the barn, got the saw, and headed for the woods. Seaborn was on my heels. He spotted a beautiful cedar and said, "Wales, let's cut this one."

It looked so tall it could touch the sky. "It's real pretty, but too big. We'll have to find a smaller one like last year," I said.

There were so many to pick from. Since we would only have a tree and probably no presents for Christmas, we wanted the prettiest one in the woods. Then we saw it. It was the most beautiful tree I had ever seen. I looked at Seaborn. He looked at me, and our hearts nearly beat out of our chests. It was a perfectly shaped cedar, just the one to catch Santa's eye.

"You hold it and push a little so I can cut it down at the bottom," I said.

I commenced to sawing so hard and fast that I had to stop every few minutes to rest and wipe the sweat off my brow. It didn't take long before our perfect tree fell. We sat down to rest. Suddenly a buck rabbit stood up in front of us. I expected it to run, but he squatted down not three feet away. I whispered, "As big as that rabbit is and as close as it is, I could kill it with a rock. But what if it has a tick on it? Ol' Black Tater told me a tick on a rabbit made the meat bad. It might poison us and we would die. I don't want to die until I know if Santa Claus will come." As we watched, the rabbit stood up, looked at both of us as if to say "Bye" and jumped into the underbrush.

It took both of us to drag the tree home. Mama was proud and helped us build a frame for it. We set it up in the front room away from the fireplace. After supper Mama, Seaborn, Robert (my 22-year-old half-brother) and I decorated it. Most all we had was crepe paper and a few glass balls with wires to hang on the limbs. We handled the balls like very precious jewels.

Long after Mama went back to finish her kitchen work, my brother and I sat in front of a roaring fire admiring our beautiful tree. We had no tree lights, but the fire light reflected on the glass balls. They twinkled like stars in the clear December night. We wanted an angel for the top but didn't have one. So we put the prettiest glass ball on the tip top. Oh, how I now wish we had known the true story of Christ's birth to comfort our little hearts.

"You reckon Santa will stop at our house?" Seaborn asked, for Santa was all we knew about Christmas.

"I suppose not. 'Cause if Mama can't get him to come, nobody can," I said. Resigned to the fact that Santa wouldn't come, we climbed up to bed a little happier than on the previous night.

A few days later, on Christmas Eve, our house smelled Christmasy. Mama had cut fresh pine boughs and red yopon berries to decorate the mantel and made a batch of oatmeal cookies. I ate at least a dozen while we sat around the big kitchen stove to keep warm. I loved to listen to the fire crackle as the wood shifted positions and burned lower. We didn't have a radio to listen to Christmas music. It was cold outside, but we had a sense of peace. Just sitting there keeping warm by the stove, eating oatmeal cookies, and being with Mama brought joy. I learned then Christmas was more than Santa Claus. It was love and family.

Mama asked, "You both full, or you want some more?"

"We're full. Thank you, Mama," we replied.

"Gettin' late. Let the fire go out and get on to bed," she said.

Once the cold began to creep into the kitchen, it didn't take much encouragement for us to head for bed.

Christmas morning, Mama called us early, "Come on down and get some hot chocolate and a pan full of buttered toast. It's mighty good when it's hot."

Our feet hit the cold floor. We grabbed our clothes, dressed, and ran out of the frigid loft.

"Reckon Santa Claus came?" my brother asked as he buttoned his shirt.

"We'll see," I whispered.

We ran into the front room where Mama was standing. She pointed to a gift she had made for my brother. Then she pointed to mine. It was an old white shoe box with four windows cut out on each side. She had pasted different colors of crepe paper over these holes. Mama had attached four empty thread spools to the box to make the front and back wheels. A long string was tied to the front of the box. She said, "Watch this," and blew out our kerosene lamp. In the middle of the shoe box was a small candle. She lit the candle and suddenly the most beautiful sight I had ever seen appeared before my eyes. It was a railroad car! I pulled it around the house all day. Every time I passed Mama I gave her a big hug and told her how much I loved her and that this was the best Christmas ever.

By the way, I almost forgot, Mama somehow managed to put a box of chocolate-covered cherries under the tree!

6
Easy Money

You boys must have gotten sick in there," Mr. Jake said as Seaborn and I emerged from the bathroom of his filling station. He took an old rag out of his hip pocket and wiped grease from his hands. The rag was so dirty it seemed to blacken his hands more.

"Why do you say that?" I asked, trying to look innocent.

"Because your mouth and lips look purple."

He was smart like Mama. He knew nobody had to use his bathroom as much as we did. We went there regularly on the pretense we needed to use the bathroom. Larceny was our real motive. A cold-drink box filled with wondrous sweet liquids rested serenely next to the rest-room door. When Mr. Jake went out to pump gas, we'd steal a Nehi Grape and duck in the men's room to gulp it down. When we came out, we thanked him for being so nice to let us use his facilities.

We were in his station one day when he received an order of candy. He told us he'd give both of us a bar if we would stack it in the show-case. We would have swept the whole station for a bar of candy! Candy had never been more lovingly or neatly stacked. He rewarded us with two chocolate bars filled with peanuts.

"This sure is good," I told him.

"You can buy two of them for a nickel."

"Two this size for a nickel?" The wheels in my mind started to turn. By morning recess, I and every kid in school were hungry. Money could be made if I had a product to sell. This was before schools sold candy, and there were no cold-drink boxes in the halls. Any boy or girl who normally didn't have friends could have them by bringing a snack.

I thought about Lucky Norman. He always had a snack for recess. His mama made the best pimento-cheese sandwiches in town. Poor

Norman couldn't enjoy his food because so many of us hung around him, envying every bite he ate.

I had figured a way to get in on Norman's snack with a promise of protection from the other boys. "But," I told him, "it'll cost you one of your Mama's pimento cheese sandwiches."

I guess he thought my help would be worth the peace gained. I knew Wallace was the oldest and toughest boy that hung on to Norman. So the next day at recess, I gave Wallace a good whipping. From then on, it was just Norman and me. In the sixth grade, I was more interested in pimento cheese sandwiches than girls.

I turned to my brother, "I bet we could sell these candy bars for a nickel a piece at school."

We worked a deal with Mr. Jake. He would let us pick up candy in the morning and settle up in the afternoon. There was one catch. We could never use his bathroom again.

Walking home, I nudged Seaborn, "Oh, well, soon we'll have money to buy our own cold drinks." We ran on, talking excitedly about all the cash we were going to make.

We carried only a few bars of candy to school at first. The word got around that we sold one whole bar of candy for only five cents. We became as popular as Norman! Best of all, I stayed out of the principal's office most of the year. I was so busy selling candy I didn't have time to get into trouble.

It wasn't long before we had to take our candy in two boxes, one for me and one for my brother. We were in big business. Mr. Jake had never sold so much candy. For one whole school year, my brother and I made lots of money. He kept his in a Prince Albert tobacco can, but I spent mine.

This job was certainly a lot easier than my first working experience. The practice of an "allowance" for children to spend any way they pleased was unheard-of during the Depression. I had to work for any money I ever hoped to have, especially since my father wasn't a giving man. "No," was his favorite word. We quit asking rather than incur his wrath.

Easy Money

I had been only eight when I started my first job delivering the
Atlanta Constitution to 60 families who lived from one end of town to
the other. The pay was 35 cents a week. To throw my papers I had to
rise with the roosters at 4:30 AM.

Mama helped me get a second-hand bike with money she earned
from washing clothes for neighbors. It cost $6 and had no rear fender.
When it rained, the back tire threw mud and dirty water all over my
back, making me look like a pole cat.

The candy business was certainly safer than delivering papers. Every
morning I had to pedal my bike down the dark street where a crazy
man lived. I wasn't afraid of anything in the world except the person
living at 1992 Moss Street. We kids named him Creamer. I'm not sure
why.

My pedals always squeaked as I rode my old blue bike down the dark
streets of the still slumbering town. It was always so peaceful to ride
along in the early morning air. That is until I came to Moss Street. The
trees crowded out the early light of the new day, and everything seemed
dark and foreboding. I would always pause to catch my breath before I
headed down that way. My heart seemed to rise to my throat making it
hard to swallow. Then, even with my heavy load of papers and my
pedals keeping a quick cadence of squeaks and shrieks, I became the
world's fastest bicycle racer. Every morning I vowed to oil my chain as I
shot like a bullet past Creamer's house.

One morning as I paused before turning onto Moss, I noticed the
light was off in Creamer's kitchen window. Other mornings, it had
always been on. I was afraid to go on and afraid not to continue my
route. If I didn't throw all my papers, I might get fired! I sat there
wondering what to tell my customers. I could say the *Constitution* had
not sent enough papers, but I knew that wouldn't work because I had
used it too many times.

Suddenly something grabbed the back of my bike and flipped me
over. Stunned, I looked up to see Creamer standing over me. He
couldn't talk; he just yelled and muttered. He wasn't big, but he looked
like a giant to me.

When I tried to get up, he pushed me down and jumped up and down and hollered gibberish at me. Buck Jones on his white horse flashed across my mind. If only Buck would come to my rescue. Instead Mr. Hubbard, our milkman, drove up. He yelled from the truck, "What's going on here?" Creamer ran away.

Mr. Hubbard jumped out of his truck, ran over to me, and asked if I was hurt. Only my pride was injured.

Yes, now I was into "easy money." Selling candy bars during recess was a heck of a lot easier than waking up at 4:30 and dodging the crazy man on Moss Street.

For the first time in my life, I couldn't wait for summer to be over. I wished for the old school bell to start ringing. We had been planning for our new fiscal year and even considered hiring other boys to help us in our business venture. But the next year was not the same. Our principal told us we couldn't sell candy anymore. The school saw how much money we had made and developed their own candy program.

It was my brother and me and who made candy the number-one selling item on campuses all across the country. The next time you see those boys or girls at a ball park with a box hung around their neck, just remember, whether our principal would own up to it or not, we Goebels started it all.

7
The Apple of God's Eye

✜

I wasn't too surprised when the big war broke out and the persecution of Jews began in Europe. I used to wonder why some people disliked the Jews and called them names. Once I heard someone call them "Christ-killers" and asked Mama what that meant. She said it didn't mean a thing. It was just the way some folks showed their ignorance. I accepted her answer, but still didn't understand.

Most everybody walked to town to work or shop. Folks lived close to the business district, so those who had cars left them at home. I used to sit in front of Baby Hat's Cafe with some friends and watch the goings and comings of the town. I remember once when Mr. Mitnick walked by, one of my friends said, "Here comes that dirty old Jew."

I said, "Yeah, those old dirty Jews," but inside my mind I was thinking, now, why did I say that? He's a lot cleaner than any of us grungy boys.

There were two Jewish families in Tallapoosa. They owned the Chevrolet dealership and were very prosperous. When the new model cars came out each year, they made it a special day and gave gifts to us kids. Mr. Mitnick knew we kids couldn't buy a car, but he never turned us away. Sometimes he gave us a mask with a rubber band on the back, or a full sack of new marbles. I'll never forget the time he gave us each a "jaw breaker." When we tucked it in our cheek, it looked like we had a good case of the mumps. When all the candy was sucked off, inside was bubble gum like none we ever had before. At night we would take it out of our mouth and leave it on the dresser. It literally lasted for days. But there were some people in town who would have burned the Chevrolet building just because it belonged to a Jew.

A whole lot of people ran pool halls and beer joints. These places weren't there to make better citizens. Many a Georgian turned to alcohol and crime by spending time at these places. No one ever talked bad about the folks who ran these dives. They only talked bad about the Jews who gave children "jaw breakers."

My awareness of people disliking Jews started in first grade. One day I was walking home from school with two buddies, and pencil-legged Harry was ahead of us. Harry was little and scrawny, but he was smarter than most of us. He kept to himself a lot, and that made him fair game for bullies.

Howard urged me and S.C. to catch up with him. Then he began punching Harry from behind until he stumbled and dropped his book. He got right up in Harry's face and jeered, "Jew baby, whatcha going to do about it?"

Harry just picked up his book and kept walking. I couldn't believe that Harry kept ignoring Howard's continual blows in his back. "Harry," I yelled, "hit him back!"

Harry didn't say a word and kept right on walking.

I got fed up with Howard and jumped between the two. "Stop! Leave him alone."

Howard turned on me, "You a Jew lover?"

"No, but I ain't no hater either."

Then came the age-old question I always hated, because it meant a fight was coming. "Whatcha gonna do about it?"

Before I knew what hit me, Howard and S.C. had me on the ground pounding my brains out. Thank goodness we were right outside Mr. Jones' bicycle-repair shop. He must have heard the ruckus because he came out and pulled them off me. They got scared and ran while Mr. Jones held me back. "Let me at 'em!" I struggled to get away from him. I wanted to return a lick or two.

"Wales, don't you know better than to jump on two brothers?" Mr. Jones asked while trying to calm me.

"I do now." I kicked a rock with my toe.

I looked for Harry, but he was long gone. Guess he figured he'd better get out of there before he received a pounding. They had given me a pretty good lickin', and Mr. Jones handed me his handkerchief. "Now what was that fight about."

"Howard was shoving Harry and calling him Jew baby. I got tired of seeing them push Harry around."

Mr. Jones looked up at the sky and was quiet. I thought, "Oh great, he doesn't like Jews either." I reached up and felt to see if my nose was still there.

Mr. Jones finally broke his silence. "You know, Wales, God especially loves the Jewish people. He says they are the apple of His eye, and Christ Himself was a Jew. I bet the Lord is proud of you for sticking up for Harry." He gave me a pat on the back like I was a big hero.

I didn't know what Mr. Jones was talking about. I thought God wasn't too fond of apples since they made Adam and Eve fall out of His good favor. If Mr. Jones thought taking up for Harry made God happy, then I'd tell Mama. She would want to know how I got my nose busted and my clothes all dirty. I thanked him and headed toward home.

The squeak of the screen door announced my arrival. Mama called, "Wales, that you, honey?"

The smell from the kitchen pulled me along like invisible fingers toward its source. Oatmeal cookies were just coming out of the oven.

"Good gracious, son, what happened to you?"

"Somebody tried to poke God's eyes out, so I made them quit," I casually replied reaching for a cookie.

"What in the world are you talking about?"

The cookie was hot and I was sucking air trying to cool my mouth. "Hawwy's God's affle."

Mama handed me a glass of milk. "I can't understand you when you talk with your mouth full."

The milk brought relief. I took a minute to gulp down a few more sips. Mama waited slightly impatiently for me to explain how I helped God.

"Mr. Jones said the Jews are God's apples. He keeps them in His eyes, and He's mighty proud of me for taking a licking for Harry." It made perfect sense to me, and it annoyed me that Mama was slow to understand. She asked who gave me the bloody nose. "It was Howard and S.C., and God's gonna sure be mad at them."

"Why will God be mad?" She still wasn't catching the meaning.

I blew on the next cookie before popping it in my mouth. "They were pushing Harry, and Harry is the apple of God's eye."

Mama wet a rag and started rubbing the blood and grime off my face. She never asked me any more about what happened. I figured she was pretty happy since God was happy with me.

Thirty years later when I went back to my high school reunion, the first place I visited was Mitnick Chevrolet. Harry had become the owner after his uncle died. He was still small. His office chair swallowed him, and seated at his desk, he looked like a kid playing in his daddy's office.

We talked awhile, then I asked if he remembered the time the two brothers beat me up when I took up for him. When he said he didn't, I was shocked. I bet he would have remembered if I had let him take the whipping S.C. and Howard gave me. But then I wouldn't have had the privilege of being God's special helper for the day.

8
Peanuts and Whiskey

✢

O ne Saturday afternoon, after losing our candy business, Seaborn and I were sitting in front of Daddy's grocery store watching the comings and goings. In the 1930s, everybody came to town on Saturday. Whole families came by horse and wagon loaded down with fresh vegetables to sell to the local merchants. School buses arrived from the more rural areas and dropped off their passengers for the day.

It was something just to watch the people who were scrubbed and combed and dressed in their best. We saw crowds lined up in front of the Grand Theater to see the triple feature. Seaborn and I didn't have money to see the show since we had lost our school candy business. Everyone going to the picture show generally bought popcorn. It hit me then that we could supply something better than popcorn!

"Seaborn, I bet we could sell those folks parched peanuts! Let's talk to Robert and see if he will help us get started."

We jumped up and ran into Daddy's store. It was hard to keep still while Robert finished waiting on a customer. We talked so fast about our idea that he said, "Hold it! One at a time." I explained our plan. "Yes, I'll help you. I'll buy the raw peanuts, and think I know where to find a second-hand peanut parcher."

The next Saturday we were set up for business. Before daylight, Seaborn and I were dipping the peanuts out of the tow sack and parching several pounds at a time. The fine aroma of parching peanuts drifted over the entire town. This was our best advertisement. When people got a whiff, they followed their noses to our peanut stand.

"Peanuts, peanuts! Get your fresh parched peanuts. Here's your peanut man." I would go hawking all around town with my old candy

41

box while Seaborn tended the machine.

Our enterprise soon doubled. We had money in our pockets and a product people wanted to buy. Good times were back again.

World War II began about this time, and the military moved a lot of troops on the Southern Railroad. The tracks went right through the middle of the business district. This changed our dealings, both for good and bad.

One Saturday morning, I was standing on the corner next to Waldrup's Drug Store with my peanut box. Business was slow because the farmers had not yet come to town. Right in front of my eyes, a troop train chugged to a steam-hissing stop. Trains had to stop in Tallapoosa to take on water.

Hundreds of soldiers hung out the windows and hollered at everybody, especially the girls. They even whistled at Mrs. McKinney, my English teacher. Now Mrs. McKinney was not the type of woman I would ever whistle at. But the soldiers did. She blushed and looked down at the ground. But then she smiled and waved back.

One soldier called me, "Boy, you got anything to eat in that box?"

"Yes sir!" I yelled back. "I've got the freshest parched Georgia peanuts you ever did see."

"Well, bring 'em over here! I'll buy every bag you've got in that box. How much are they?"

We sold them to the town folks for five cents, but I raised the price. "Ten cents a bag," I answered without batting an eye.

"How many bags you got?" he asked.

"Twenty."

He handed me $2.00, and I gave him all I had.

Another soldier called out, "You got any more?"

Our machine was only a block away. I ran like the wind and told Seaborn to bring all he had and follow me. The train just stayed 20 minutes. We sold out. Hundreds of soldiers kept asking for more.

Selling parched peanuts suddenly became big business in Tallapoosa. We met every train. When the trains left, so would our peanuts, and our pockets were stuffed with money.

One day after I sold all my peanuts, a soldier called me over to the window. "I'll give you a quarter to run across the street to that cafe and get me a ham sandwich." I dashed across the street and nearly knocked a customer over who was coming out the door. The waitress rushed up the sandwich, and I sprinted back to the train. I asked if anybody else wanted a sandwich. I would get it for a 25-cent delivery fee. They all started pushing money at me, but the engineer blew his whistle. I watched the soldiers as the train pulled out, not sure who was more disappointed, them or me.

Seaborn and I convinced the depot operator to tell us the troop trains' schedules. The moving of troops was normally secret, but not from us. We learned they came through town at all hours of the day and night. To meet the demand for sandwiches, we hired our friends to help.

Our business got so big, the merchants complained to the mayor. The city council supported us, but to pacify the merchants, we had to buy a license.

We sold hundreds of sandwiches, and made a bundle for ourselves and our friends. We didn't mind the 2:00 AM train because we were making so much money. We should have been satisfied, but greener pasture loomed ahead. One of our helpers told me how we could really make big bucks. His daddy was a bootlegger and could get white whiskey to sell to the soldiers. This was a long time before my encounter with the sheriff. I liked the idea, and after a whispered conversation with the other boys, we decided to try it.

A few days later, we had several gallons of moonshine poured up in pint bottles. Some of us slapped the sandwiches together. Others poured the whiskey into the bottles.

I don't guess I'll ever forget how nervous I was the first time we sold whiskey to the troops. We were afraid to sell to the day trains. It was safer at night. We put the pints in the bottom of our boxes and covered them with sandwiches.

In spite of it being after midnight, we were wide-awake waiting for the train. When we heard it chugging up the tracks, my mouth got dry and chalky. I thought maybe I should have a chug out of one of the pints. The black steel engine glided slowly through the darkness with the brakes grinding metal on metal until it came to a halt in front of the water tower. The hissing steam swirled around the engine. It looked like a restless spirit in the eerie glow of the train's headlight that shone directly on the tracks.

We boys took a quick look at each other, then ran along the side of the cars and hollered, "Good, hot sandwiches for sale!"

The trains were not air-conditioned so the windows were open. Sleepy soldiers soon appeared. "How much?" they asked.

"Thirty-five cents."

"Gimme two," most would say.

"You can have three hams for one dollar."

A dollar would come down in a hand and three sandwiches would go back up. Another soldier woke up and asked, "What's going on out there?" The answer came, "Some kids selling sandwiches, three hams for one dollar." The new customer leaned out the window and said, "Gimme three."

When we sold out of sandwiches, I said, "How would you like to have a pint of the best whiskey made, not only in Georgia, but the whole world?"

It seemed as if every soldier all the way up and down the train awoke and leaned out the windows, "Boy! don't you sell all that whiskey until you get to me!" they yelled. One soldier asked, "How much whiskey you got in that box?"

"Ten pints."

"How much?" he asked.

"Three dollars a pint."

"Naw! I mean for all of it," he said.

"Thirty dollars."

"Hand it up here, boy."

I said, "No, sir. You hand down the thirty dollars."

Another soldier called, "Boy, you bring that whiskey over here." But three ten-dollar bills landed in my box. I handed up the whiskey. When the train pulled out, I could still hear the soldiers fussing over our whiskey.

Just as in the candy business, peanut, and now ham sandwich business, we had plans to get bigger and make more money. I didn't think of the consequences of our selling whiskey. Dollar bills blinded me. We sold as much whiskey to the troops as we could carry in our boxes.

One morning I woke up exhausted from the previous night's lack of sleep. I stumbled down the steps from the loft and slunk into the kitchen. Over breakfast I asked Mama if I could quit school. I figured I could make all the money I would ever need, so why go to school? Now Mama never knew about the whiskey. She would have skinned me alive with a switch right then and there. I was more afraid of *her* catching me than the law.

Our hangout was Mrs. Cole's Cafe, and I was in there counting my money one afternoon when the chief of police, Mr. Slaughter, came in. He called me aside. I quickly stuffed the bills into my back pocket and walked over to his table. "What you boys selling to those soldiers on the train?" he asked.

"Why," I said piously, "fresh hot ham sandwiches."

"What else, Wales?"

"Why, that's all," I said. "What do you think we sell?"

He didn't answer, but just left his coffee sitting there and walked out. I told my friend, Wayne, about the conversation, and we agreed to sell only sandwiches for a while. We did for a week, but it wasn't fun anymore, and our green-back roll shrank. So we went back to selling whiskey.

We got so brave we would take our whiskey on board the train and walk through the cars selling. We'd ride the train to Waco where a steep grade caused the train to slow down. Then we jumped off and rode back to Tallapoosa with one of our helpers who picked us up in a car.

I did not heed the police chief's warning, but the good times still came to an end. My second warning came when I heard the Army had come to Tallapoosa to investigate our business. All the law enforcement officers, county and city, were on alert. I thought about Mama. It would kill her if she found out.

I decided to go back to ham sandwiches only. I can't say it was easy money we made. We worked hard, and we were available at all hours.

One afternoon we boys were lolling on the benches outside the station waiting for a train. Out of nowhere came a dozen green Army vehicles filled with MPs and our own three policemen. They searched us but found only ham sandwiches.

By being greedy, we lost it all. The army would no longer let us sell sandwiches to the trains.

Most of us boys loitered on the station's benches and watched the trains come and go wishing we could still sell to the troops. Sometimes just for fun, I'd ask a soldier, "Would you like to buy a ham sandwich?"

Two or three would lean out the windows, and one would ask, "How much?"

"Thirty-five cents."

"Gimme one. Do you have any spirits, too?"

Little did I know that years later I'd be preaching about Jesus who could give eternal life and fill those who believed with the Living Spirit.

9
Big Red

I awoke long before sunrise with a sense of doom heavier than the quilts covering me. This was the worst day of all my ten years. I pulled the quilts up to my chin and dreaded the sound of Mama's call. I wished this day would just go away.

I loved autumn. The frost had killed the kudzu and all the trees' leaves were red and gold. The crisp mornings made me jump quickly from the warm bed into my clothes. It would soon be Thanksgiving and then Christmas.

This morning, pain filled my heart, because this was the day Robert was going to butcher Big Red. I was just six when we bought Big Red from a neighbor. I toted her home in my arms. I played with her like she was a pet dog. She followed me around the yard until she got so big we had to build a pen for her. Most people think pigs are ugly, but to me Big Red was a beauty.

When Mama called me to come to breakfast, I answered, "Yes, ma'am." I slept in my long-handle underwear, so I just had to slip on my flannel shirt, a pair of pants, then pull my overalls on. I headed down to the warm kitchen quickly.

"Wash your hands and face. Your oatmeal is good and hot," Mama said.

Robert came in wearing the same old clothes he always wore when he slaughtered one of the animals.

"Old Big Red looked mighty unhappy yesterday," I said.

"That old pig doesn't know anything, and besides, when I put a bullet between its eyes, she won't feel a thing." Robert was trying to reassure me. He knew I was sad and sick at heart.

"How do you know she won't feel anything?" My lower lip quivered.

"Animals don't have feelings like humans," he replied. "They don't know pain."

"How do you know?" I asked with a trembling voice.

"I just know. That's how I know" was his answer.

"It's a funny thing, when Red got her leg caught in the fence, she squealed until she got free," I countered.

"She was just scared," Robert said. "Pigs have a tendency to get scared."

Robert drank a cup of Mama's coffee while waiting for me to finish breakfast.

"You're eatin' mighty slow this morning. Hurry up and let's go," he said.

I looked out the window. Tater and old Joe were coming across the field. These two black men were friends of Robert and were going to help.

"Take this slop out to Big Red," Mama said. "She'll be hungry. Wales, your pig will be all right."

"Yes, ma'am." I wondered how Big Red was going to be "all right" dead.

Big Red was so excited to see me. She nearly knocked the bucket out of my hands. I fed her twice a day. She always ate whatever I put in her trough. I scratched behind her leathery old ears and spoke to her reassuringly. "It won't hurt, Red. Robert said you don't feel like people do." She just kept her head in the trough and went right on eating.

Robert's call broke into my time with Red. "Come draw up some well water and fill the wash pots."

Tater and Joe were making a fire under the pots as I drew the water to fill them. I sat on a wooden cola box and watched the flames shoot sparks out from under the old iron pots.

Tater, Joe, and Robert sat across from me with a half gallon of moonshine. This is how Robert got his two black friends to help. They passed the jar between them and drank a whole half gallon without getting drunk.

When steam rose above the water and bubbles popped on the

surface, Robert started to the pig pen. "You stay here, Wales," he told me. "Joe, Tater, and I will get Big Red."

"Robert, please don't kill Big Red," I begged.

"What do you mean, boy, don't kill Big Red? What will you do for pork chops you like so much? Where will you get that good ham your Mama cooks for breakfast? Where're you gonna get good sausage? And what about the chitlin's for ol' Joe and Tater?"

"I don't want any more pork chops. I'll never eat ham if you won't kill Big Red." I wiped away tears leaving streaks of dirt across my cheeks.

"You sit by the fire. We'll be back shortly," he said.

"Are you going to kill Big Red?" I asked.

"That's right. I'm going to kill Big Red. Don't you know God made animals so humans could eat them? Now you don't wanta make God mad, do you?"

I couldn't conceive of God getting mad just because I didn't want to kill Big Red.

Soon I heard the squeals. I knew Tater and Joe were in the pen getting a rope around her neck. Even with my fingers stuck in my ears and pressing my hands against the side of my head, I couldn't shut out the sound of Red squealing.

They loaded her in the back of Robert's old Dodge truck and brought her to the slaughter place.

"If you shoot her, I'll shoot your headlights out with my Buck Jones air rifle," I screamed.

Robert put his rifle on his shoulder. Tater took one end of Big Red and old Joe got the other. They held her down until she couldn't move. It seemed she just gave up. She quit squealing.

"Go on up to the house," Robert ordered.

I begged one last time.

"Git! Git now or I will shoot her while you're standing here," Robert yelled.

I ran away as fast as I could, passing Mama in the kitchen. I crawled under her bed. "Bang!" My heart jumped. I buried my head in my hands and sobbed. Mama had to call me out.

"Where you going with your air rifle?" Mama asked.

"To shoot some cans," I lied.

I walked down to where old Red was hanging. Robert was cutting her up. He saw me coming and said, "Go on back to the house and help your Mama."

I didn't say a thing, but walked to the front of Robert's truck. I pumped my air rifle and shot out his left front light. Before he reached me, I had pumped again and shot out his right light.

"What the devil is wrong with you?" Robert bellowed. He grabbed my air rifle and wrapped it around a tree.

"Get out of here before I break your neck!" he yelled.

I walked back into the kitchen and Mama asked, "Where's your rifle?"

"Robert broke it," I said.

"Why?" she asked puzzled.

"Because I shot out the headlights of his truck."

"In heaven's name, why would you do that?" she asked.

"Because he killed Big Red."

Robert was one of my favorite half-brothers, and I knew he loved me. I found out early in life, way before I learned what the Bible says about forgiveness, when you know someone loves you, no matter what they have done, it's not hard to forgive. I forgave Robert.

A couple of weeks later, I came in from school and noticed something sticking out from under my bed. I lay down on my belly to look and see what it was. I couldn't believe my eyes. I reached out to feel it just to make sure. Then slowly, reverently, I pulled out a brand new Buck Jones air rifle! A note was attached to it, "From Robert, for Big Red."

10
Sweet Shrubs and Death

Now that we weren't selling ham sandwiches, I liked to go to the train station and watch the local boys leaving for the war. Every day a family sent their boy off to fight in places most of us had never heard of. They kissed their mamas and girl friends and shook their papa's hand. Sometimes there was an emotional hug between a son and father. The family stood on the platform hugging and crying until the conductor signaled the engineer. The boy leaving then leaned out the window as far as he could, looking back and waving till the train chugged out of sight.

No matter how many trains pulled away from the station, whether it was kin folks, friends, or a total stranger, the whole town felt a part of us was leaving. I always wondered if the fellow leaving would come back. Some didn't. I couldn't totally understand the pain since my closest relative who went off to war was an uncle who lived in Birmingham.

My uncle was stationed at an army base near home. The army made him a sergeant since he had been in the service before. He had short passes and often came to see us. I looked forward to meeting his train. My chest bulged with pride, and I threw my shoulders back as I carried his bag to our house. Walking beside him when he was dressed up in his uniform made me feel kinda like I was a soldier, too. I surely planned to be one. Everybody but me wanted the war to end. I couldn't wait for my birthdays to pass so I could join up.

My friend P.J. and I played war games after school every day. We talked about how many Japs we'd kill. We'd have no mercy on them after Pearl Harbor. We had watched "Bataan" and "Guadalcanal Diary" at least a dozen times. Those two picture shows made us ready to fight.

Our machine guns were made out of scrap lumber. They didn't look like much, and folks would never recognize them as guns. To us they were the finest the military issued its troops. We ran all over the pasture behind our house and killed thousands of Japs.

Sometimes the fog would settle over the pasture behind our house. That made perfect fighting conditions. We ran as fast as we could, the tall grass slapping our legs making a hiss, hissing with every stride.

"Drop!" I'd shout to P.J. We both immediately dove into the thick grass. The only noise was the sound of our heavy breathing. The mist was our cover as we crawled on our bellies peering through the lush vegetation. I held my arm up to signal our halt.

"What'cha see?" P.J. whispered. Frantically I waved my arm to keep him quiet and stay low. Holding my gun close to my body, I rolled over to him and whispered, "Japs!" His eyes grew wide as saucers. "Must be a couple hundred." My heart thumped in my chest with anticipation.

P.J. was always sure of himself. "Is that all?" He looked a little scornful.

I lifted my head above the grass, then ducked quickly, dodging a bullet. "Well, maybe three hundred." I revised my estimate.

"Over there." I pointed to some trees. "Let's surround them." We jumped up and ran to the cover of the trees and started shooting. Back to back, we faced our enemy. "Pow, pow, bang, bang, bang." I grabbed a pine cone from my pocket, put it to my mouth, and pulled out the stem. "Kerblam!!" I yelled as it sailed from my hand and blew up at least 200 of the enemy.

"I'm hit!" P.J. hollered and sank dramatically to the ground. "Bam, bam, bam." I shot as I reached down to put my arm around P.J. Like true marines, we always rescued each other. "You'll make it," I assured him. "I won't let them get you like they did General Wainwright and his troops in the Philippines." I kept firing back as I pulled him limping along to the back steps of our house.

"Where are you hurt?" I examined him after we reached the safety zone.

"My hands," he grimaced. "I shot so many Japs my gun got hot, so hot it burned the skin off my hands." He rolled over, writhing in agony. I ran inside to find the medals. When I came out, I turned to the "other troops." "Attention!" I shouted to them. Then helping P.J. stand up on the bottom step, I pinned the Purple Heart I had cut out of board paper from school on his shirt with some of Mama's safety pins. I stepped back and gave him my salute which, of course, he returned even though his hands were badly injured.

"Well, I better get home now, Wales."

"See you at school tomorrow." I waved after him as he ran down the road toward home.

I remember as if it were yesterday when the Helton boy left for the war. Like all the country boys, he came to town for schooling. His daddy was a farmer, and by doing heavy farm work after school and on weekends, he developed big arms and wide shoulders. He was two years older than me, and I looked up to him because he was an all-American type guy. The teachers wished all their students were like him, for he was quiet and serious in his school work.

One thing about those boys raised out in the country, none became alcoholics, committed suicide, divorced, or even made poor grades in school. Another thing I saw in them, and longed for, was they all seemed closer as families.

Church was as much a part of their life as school and plowing. They all went to church. There was nothing else to do. Their folks were generally too poor to own a radio, and we didn't have TV in the forties. The newspapers were not delivered out in the country, so going to church was the big event of the week.

These rural families would get together after church, bring their meals to one house, and have a real feast. Grown-ups ate first, while the kids played out in the yard. When the adults were through, the kids would have their turn.

The leftover food was put on one table with a tablecloth spread over it to keep flies off. The food stayed on the table all afternoon. Anyone was free to go and help himself. By evening church time, most of the food had been eaten.

The women sat on the front porch in rocking chairs and talked. The men, along with the young children, would find a chair, couch, or bed to take a snooze. The older boys and girls would get up a game of soft-ball out in the pasture.

There would always be a couple sweet on each other, and they got off somewhere alone. They couldn't stay away long, for the mamas on the porch watched to see who was missing. They would holler their names. You'd see the two walk out of the woods like they didn't know one another. The mama would say to her daughter, "You children stay out here where we can see you, you hear?"

"Yes, ma'am," the boy would reply.

"We're going to have to be leaving for church pretty soon. You might as well walk on toward the house."

"Yes, ma'am," the girl would answer, looking over her shoulder longingly to her sweetheart.

This way of living is lost today. I never knew of a girl who became pregnant out of wedlock. Venereal disease was as unspoken as the Chinese language.

When I dated a country girl and we wanted to sit on the front porch, my girl would have to go tell her mama where she was going. Her mama would give permission but say, "Don't go any further than the front porch and turn the light on."

"Oh, Mama! It'll just draw the bugs."

Her mama would hand me a fly swatter.

The Heltons unloaded out of two pickup trucks and one car at the train station. I spoke to everyone and fell in with the family like I was a member.

Everybody was laughing and talking until the whistle of Number Seven sounded at the dangerous crossing in Cotton Mill Town three miles away. It was like a voice reminding the family of the gravity of the setting. Everyone fell silent as they listened to it echo down the tracks.

I'll never forget the face of that mama as she stood there looking at her boy. The daddy walked up, placed his weather-worn hand on the boy's shoulder. His eyes were moist, tears on the brim of his lids, but they didn't dare spill over. He must be strong for his family.

The train chugged slowly around the curve at Hilderbrand's drug store. "Here it comes, Papa." A child's little voice broke the anxious silence.

The brakes screeched and steam hissed as the train rolled to a stop. The next few moments were like a wake. Everyone hugged, some sobbed, but mostly everyone was quiet.

The conductor called, "All aboard!"

The big steam engine had taken on all the water it needed till Atlanta. The boy looked at his daddy. Their eyes met in quiet understanding, and their gaze lingered on the other's face as if trying to memorize every line or wrinkle. Finally the father opened his arms and held his son in a strong, loving embrace.

Normally the conductor would look at his watch and call "All aboard" again. Today keeping a schedule was not as important as the ordeal this family was suffering.

At last the boy turned to his mama. He put his hand on her cheek, wiping the tears off with his thumb. She was a poor, dirt farmer's wife dressed in homemade clothes. A little white crocheted shawl draped her shoulders, and black shoes laced up past her ankles. But she was a lady and beautiful.

One uncle took off his hat and said, "Let's pray."

I was shocked to see what happened next. Right there on the platform, in broad daylight, the family bowed their heads. The conductor even took off his hat, and folks all around got quiet. The prayer that was prayed right then and there by the train in the middle of Tallapoosa, Georgia, was the most beautiful thing I'd ever heard. I got up real close because I had always wanted to learn a prayer. Time seemed to stand still until the "Amen" was uttered. Everything came back to life as if it had held its breath during the solemn moment.

"Write home as soon as you get settled in," his mama said as she walked to the train door with her arm around her son. His daddy carried his suitcase.

"Yes, ma'am," he said.

"We all love you, and we're gonna pray every day until God brings you back to us."

Mama and son hugged once more. Everybody cried, even the dad. What's more, I cried.

As he stepped up on the little stairs of the train, I hollered at him and went up and shook his hand. I told him not to worry. I would be coming over in a couple of years. P.J. too.

I was in the pool hall when the Jackson boy walked in. He scanned the room without saying anything. All the men and boys there knew something was wrong. He took a deep breath and blurted out, "The Heltons just got word from the army. Their boy has been killed."

Something left me. A great emptiness came crowding into my heart. I wanted to holler and I wanted to cry, but we all just laid our cue sticks down. I walked out of the pool hall in a daze. I remembered the family saying good-by. I couldn't believe he was gone. Dead. My emotions were overwhelming.

I wanted to do something for them, but what? I had no money. Then I remembered how much Mama loved the sweet shrub's blossoms I'd bring her. They grew wild down by the slaughter-pen bridge on the road to the Helton's house.

I jumped on my old bike and pedaled down to the bridge. My brakes squealed as I pulled up to a stop. I left the bike by the side of the road and climbed down the bank to the stream below. The rushing of the water was soothing to my troubled soul. The sweet smell of the shrubs permeated the air in the cool dark of the woods. I wanted to sit and enjoy the solitude, but the memory of Mrs. Helton's face beckoned me to hurry.

I picked as many blooms as my sack would hold and climbed back up to the road. My old bike still didn't have a rear fender, but it had a good chain and tires. The Helton farm was several miles out, but I thought the sweet shrubs would somehow help Mrs. Helton.

I rode up to the house and saw Mr. Helton sitting on the porch with two men. He didn't know me. I told him I was one of the Goebel boys.

He asked if I was Vic's son. I told him, "No, sir. A.G. Goebel is my daddy."

"The old man's your father?"

"Yes, sir," I replied.

"What can we do for you, son?" he asked.

"I was in school with your boy. He was older, but we ate chili at Baby Hat's Cafe together. I was with you all when he got on the train." I replied.

"Oh, won't you come in?" he said.

"Thank you, sir."

Then he asked, "What'cha got in the bag?"

"It's something for Mrs. Helton. I pick them for my Mama at times. She loves to smell them. I thought Mrs. Helton would like them, too."

She walked out on the porch. It was an awful sight to see a mama grieving for her dearly loved son. I thought, what if this ever happened at my house? I sure hoped it would be me. I couldn't bear to see Mama hurt because of the death of a son.

She asked me to come in.

The house was small with rooms even smaller than ours. But just like Mama, what little she had she kept neat as a pin. In the living room on the wall hung a picture of her son. Underneath was a gold star. As she stopped to admire it, she pointed out how handsome he was.

She asked me to sit at her kitchen table. She said, "Since you rode all the way from town, you must be thirsty."

"Yes, ma'am," I said. "I could do with a little water."

She asked, "How about a glass of cold, fresh milk?"

I said, "That'd be fine."

Farm folks always have a cake. They keep one for themselves and for drop-in company.

She said, "Tell me how big a piece you'd like."

"As big as you want to cut it," I said.

It was a chocolate cake like Mama bakes and was almost as good.

"Did you know my son?" she asked.

"Yes, ma'am, at school. He was older, but he was nice to us younger boys. There was something Christian about him I wanted for myself," I answered.

She said, "He was a good boy. Never caused us a minute of trouble. Well, what's in your bag?"

I said, "Well, ma'am, as I told Mr. Helton, my Mama loves sweet shrubs and I thought you might, too. Mama puts them in a handkerchief, wraps it real tight, and ties it with a string. She puts them in her dress pockets, then when she wants, she takes them out and smells their sweet smell."

She asked, "You rode all the way out here to bring me those?"

"Yes, ma'am," I said. "I did it because of what happened to your boy. When I go off to war and get killed, I would hope somebody would keep bringing sweet shrubs to Mama."

She hugged me and then cried.

I rode out of her yard onto the red clay road that would lead me home. "Yes sir," I thought, "if I get killed, I sure hope somebody will take Mama some sweet shrubs. And I know she'd give them a glass of sweet milk and a piece of chocolate cake that's the best that was ever made."

11
The Paddle or the Belt?

For me in grammar school, Fridays were never "Thank God it's Friday." Most of the students at ole' Tallapoosa Elementary were happy to see the end of the week. Some of us, usually boys, looked on it with fear and trembling for that was the day Mr. Duncan visited our school. He walked the block from the high school where he was principal to administer "discipline." I can't remember getting a whipping from any lady teacher. They left it to Mr. Duncan.

I never forgot Mr. Duncan's "lessons" and wish they had changed me on the inside the way I was later transformed. I would have avoided most of the mess that nearly ruined my life. Don't get me wrong, he never misused his authority. His punishment was meant to put enough fear of the consequence of misbehaving to keep us out of trouble so we'd become good citizens.

Every Friday morning at 9:45, Mrs. Brock, my sixth-grade teacher, called out the names alphabetically of the boys to meet with Mr. Duncan. When she got to the "G's" my hands would sweat and I'd get dizzy.

"Tootie Row Gable," she droned on impassively.

"Please don't call my name, please don't call my name," I whispered to myself with eyes closed and fists clenched. I opened my eyes when she paused and looked up hopefully. Our eyes met and she smiled as if to say "I'm going to have mercy on Wales." But then she bellowed out my name where all the school could hear, and maybe most in Tallapoosa.

I don't know exactly how a person about to be executed feels, but at that moment my feelings were as close as I cared to come.

The whole class would sit there: those to be whipped, those who felt sorry for us, and those who were glad we were about to get it. It was more like a wake. I watched the hands of the old railroad clock that hung in our room—9:55, 9:56, 9:57. Three more minutes. I asked if I could get a glass of water.

Mrs. Brock answered, "NO."

At 10:00 AM the bell rang. It sounded louder than it ever did for recess, lunch, or the end of the school day. Up and down the hall, the doors flew open like jail cells on the "Rock" at Alcatraz. We condemned boys got up from our desks and walked into the hall. I looked back at my friends for pity. Twice I looked at Mary Jo Walton, my sixth-grade sweetheart. I knew she cared for me if nobody else in school did.

At least 20 boys walked down the hall to an empty room, the last door on the left. This room was never used for a classroom. Its purpose, for all I remember, was to act as Mr. Duncan's "torture chamber."

I surveyed my fellow sufferers. Bill caught my eye and smiled weakly. Was he remembering our original encounter with the principal?

That memory of my very first day in school was as vivid as if it had happened the day before. I was up and dressed before Mama called. She had made me a new shirt and bought me new boots. She tucked a #.2 pencil in my overalls' pocket, handed me a sack lunch, and walked with me to the front porch. She said, "You look as handsome as Prince Albert." I wondered who he was but knew I looked good. Seaborn stood on the porch holding Mama's hand and asked why he couldn't go to school, too.

My heart raced with excitement when I saw the school grounds filled with kids. Bill, who was starting first grade, and his brother, plus a bunch of older boys, were standing near the swings. He called me over because the older boys egged him on to pick a fight with me. He was big with broad shoulders for a six-year-old. To provoke me, he asked if I would share my lunch at recess.

I said, "What if I don't?"

He curled his finger up one at a time making a fist and waved it in my face, "I'll whip you then."

"OK, I'll share." We had never had a fight, and I wasn't sure I could beat him.

"Ha! I'm gonna whip you anyway." Bill laughed, glancing around for approval from the older boys.

I knew, if my clothes got messed up or my new shirt got torn, it would be worse for me at home. I stood still for about a second watching him laugh. Then, without a word, I hit him as hard as I could in the mouth. Blood gushed from his smashed lips, and he let out a yell the whole town could hear.

The older boys ran and told a teacher what I had done. I knew I was in trouble when she came out. It was a bad omen to be sent to the principal's office the first hour of the first day of first grade! That office became my second homeroom all through the rest of my time in school.

Our principal, Mr. Jones, was the biggest man I ever saw. I tried to explain my side, but he had already decided my verdict was guilty from the teacher's report. "Go outside, Wales, and cut me some switches from that big bush by my office window." His tone of voice made me shake in my boots. Later, I learned this bush was called the "Jones Bush."

When I walked out of the office to go cut my switch I saw big boys, little boys, and all sizes of girls going every which away to their classes. A little red-headed girl asked if I knew where the first-grade room was.

I said, "No."

"Come on, and I'll show you."

I followed her instead of going for the switch. Our teacher assigned me to a little chair around a square table with six other boys. All day I watched the door for Mr. Jones. Every time the teacher called my name, my heart nearly stopped, but he never came. Guess he had other boys who had done worse than me.

I wished Mr. Duncan would forget about me now, but this time Bill and I would take our licks together.

We heard the front door downstairs open and close. The sound was similar to the jailhouse doors I would hear later. We could hear Mr. Duncan walking up the steps. We knew his gait. He was a polio victim

as a young man and walked with a limp. His slow, irregular, loud
thumps on the steps sounded like Frankenstein in the movies we saw at
the Grand Theater.

He always paused at the top of the stairs to get his breath. Silently,
he looked us over. One hand held a couple of paddles and the other,
two belts.

"You boys line up against the wall in alphabetical order," he commanded, waving the belts in the direction of the wall.

I wished my name started with an "A." Listening to the licks of
those in front of me was almost as bad as the real thing. As my turn got
closer, I wanted to run. By the sixth grade, I had been in that room too
many times. Each time I would swear I would never come back. If I ran,
where would I go? I was too young for the Marines. I couldn't go to
other folks' homes because they would just take me directly to Mama.

I felt like a possum up a tree. When we hunted possums, they would
climb to the highest limb on a tree and go as far out as possible. Our
dogs would surround the base of the tree and bark and jump as high as
they could trying to catch the possum. They would make such a racket
we had no trouble catching up with them. We would shine flashlights
on the possums. You could see fear in the little critters' eyes. I knew
now how the possum felt.

I made a pledge in that hall that as long as I lived, I would never
climb another tree and shake the limb until the poor helpless possum
fell to the ground.

"You want the paddle or the belt?" Mr. Duncan asked.

I felt my "limb" being shook. It was like asking, "Do you want the
electric chair or the rope?" I had the belt last time, so I chose the
paddle.

"Lean over the desk."

I knew the position to take, but he said it anyway to keep in the
rhythm of things.

"Pull your pants close to your legs. You got on more than one pair?"
"No, sir."

I knew better. Some boys would wear two or three pairs of pants on

Friday. Nobody ever got away with it. They'd get extra licks. And one more lick than you were already due was one too many.

Mr. Duncan never drew blood nor left marks. He had perfected the fine art of tearing up your behind without that. But you knew you had been whipped and whipped good.

Betty Jo called me years later and asked me to our 1940s school reunion. All the classes that graduated in the '40s were invited. I counted the days to go back home and see old friends. When the day arrived, we all tried to best each other in how well we'd done since leaving old Tallapoosa High.

I easily recognized my teachers. It seemed they never really aged. They looked old when I was their student!

Myra, Jo, Jean, Betty, Francis, Barbara, and a few others reminded me that I had promised to marry each of them. We hugged, laughed, and shed tears. After looking me up and down, they were more satisfied with the men they *had* married.

I asked, "Where's Mr. Duncan?" One of the girls pointed to a corner. He'd had brain surgery and couldn't stand. Dozens of boys who used to stand in that hall line with me stood around him. Some hugged him. Others shook his hand.

When I walked over, he looked up and recognized me.

"Hello, Mr. Duncan."

"You want the paddle or the belt?" he asked with a twinkle in his eye.

I reached around and hugged his neck, and he did mine.

I whispered, "Thank you."

I'm not sure he heard me. He never responded verbally. He just patted me on the back.

"Mr. Duncan, I turned out to be a pretty good boy."

"You always were," he said. "You just got carried away every once in a while. I never doubted for a minute about you, Wales. I knew your Mama would see to that."

I hate to think what kind of trouble I would have gotten into even in grammar school if Mr. Duncan hadn't been there.

12
It's A Man's Job

had to find another way to make money after the police and Army stopped my booming business of selling sandwiches and moonshine. Mr. Evans gave me a job delivering groceries. Every morning I called on homes and took grocery orders. When Mr. Evans filled the orders, I hopped on my bicycle and delivered them. The store's pickup truck was used only for heavy deliveries since gas was rationed because of the war.

Back then in Tallapoosa, we never locked our doors. I just opened the screen door and walked right through the house to the kitchen. The groceries went on the table and the meat and milk in the icebox. Most folks kept homemade cookies or a cake on their kitchen counter. I'd always call out to whoever lived there and asked if it would be all right to take some cookies. They'd call back, "Didn't you get some this morning?"

"No, ma'am. It was probably the ice man."

"Oh, all right," they would say, "but just take what you can in your hands. Don't put any in your pocket."

The conversation would go on and nobody ever came into the kitchen. I'd leave the bill on the table, and the lady of the house would come by the store during the week and pay Mr. Evans.

When I'd get back to the store, Mr. Evans would look at my bulging overalls pocket and ask, "What you got in there?"

"Cookies," I'd say without a blink from my conscience.

I was 14 and would rather have joined the Marines than call on homes to get grocery orders. Each week as more of the older boys left for the Army or Navy, the war changed me. For the first time in my life, I began to feel a sense of pride. It wasn't the Grand Old Flag or patriotism. It was the girls who changed me.

I had always been tall for my age. In my first-grade class picture I was the tallest. As a high-school freshman, I had reached the height of six feet, one inch. I wasn't skinny nor did I have "Charles Atlas" muscles. Just muscular. If I ever caught up to my size 12D feet, no telling how tall I would be. Every time my Aunt Eunice saw me, she'd say, "You sure are big for your age." I was taller than her husband when he went off to war.

It never mattered one way or another about being tall until the older boys left for the service. Suddenly, girls began making a play for me. I don't mean the girls in my class at school, but older girls in junior and senior high.

I was about the biggest boy around, except for the "4-F's," and they were no competition. The girls looked at them as disabled, because they were disqualified from going to the war for one reason or another.

My first experience with a girl happened one Saturday afternoon. The meat cutter told me to take an order of hamburger to the Friendly Cafe on Head Avenue.

I picked up the sack of meat and pedaled to the cafe. The girl behind the counter was a senior, and her mama and papa owned the place. She had a reputation for dating older men.

"Where do you want me to put the hamburger meat?" I asked.

"In the ice box," she waved her hand in the direction of the kitchen.

The kitchen wasn't as clean as the serving area. There was no air conditioning then, and it was awfully hot back there. A small fan hummed quietly on the counter, but it only stirred the warm air.

"You might as well turn it off," I nodded at the fan. "It ain't doing any good."

"Mama turns it on when she's cooking," she answered. "Leave it on. She thinks it does some good."

"Boy, it's sure hot in here. I don't see how your mama can stay in this place. Aren't you hot?"

"Burning up," she said and rubbed a piece of ice over her lips. It was her eyes that disturbed me. She lowered her lids and let her fingers run slowly through her hair, lifting it off her shoulders.

"I'd better get back to the store," I said and started to leave.

"No, sir," she said. "You go right out to the counter, sit on a stool, and I'll bring you a big glass of lemonade."

"I should be going," I answered.

"Why, they aren't going to miss you in the next five minutes." She actually winked at me.

I was nervous, for her eyes seemed glued on me. Dreamy like. But I did want the lemonade, so I obediently sat on the end stool at the counter. She came out of the kitchen with a huge glass full of iced lemonade. It made me cool just looking at it. The girl set it in front of me and put her elbows on the counter, cupped her face in her hands and smiled. I'd never had a girl look at me that way before. In a way I was frightened.

"Are those homemade cookies?" I asked, turning away from her toward a cake stand with a glass cover.

"A lady in town makes them," she answered.

"I'll bet one of them would be good with this big ol' glass of lemonade," I said.

"The lemonade is free. The cookie costs a nickel. How many do you want?"

"One," I said. "No, make it two. Then I'll owe you a dime."

After I had eaten the cookies, I realized I had made a big mistake. The cookies were gone, and I didn't have a dime.

"I'll try to pay you next week," I said.

"You can pay me right now if you want to," she whispered and moved a little closer to my face.

"How?" I asked. "I'm broke."

"By helping me move the chest of drawers out of my bedroom into the hall," she said and kept giving me that "look."

She lived in an apartment above the cafe.

"Can I move it all by myself?" I asked.

"No, but I'll help."

"What about the cafe?"

"I'll just lock the door. It'll only take a minute."

"I don't know," I said, trying to figure how to get out of there.

"Why, with your big ole' arms, it won't take two minutes," she said and leaned across the counter and stroked my shoulder.

I looked at my muscles and thought, "She sees something I don't."

"Let me feel that muscle," she said sliding her hand down my arm.

"O.K., come on. Let's go move the chest, but then I must be goin', or Mr. Evans might fire me." Her touch made me restless. I stood up to try to calm myself.

"I bet you must be 18. Why aren't you in the Army?" she asked.

"I'm 14 and three-fourths."

"You're kidding," she said. "You passed 14 four years ago."

"Do I look that old?" I asked, swelling up and feeling proud.

"You look older than my brother, and he was 19 when he went to the war," she said. "He wasn't near your size. I bet you have to fight the girls off."

"Well, they get a little carried away sometimes," I tried to act indifferent. I was as good a liar as she was. But for a boy of only 14 and three-fourths, I enjoyed hearing her talk to me that way.

"When are you gonna let me feel that muscle in your arm?" she asked, walking around the counter toward me.

I strained to make my muscle larger as I bent my elbow. She moved closer to me and squeezed my arm. "Oh, my goodness, no boy in my senior class has a muscle that big," she gushed.

That girl had me believing I had an arm like a blacksmith. She led me up the stairs, but stopped in the middle of her living room, turned slowly, and faced me. "You ever kiss girls?"

"Yeah, sometimes. Where's the chest of drawers you want moved?" I looked over her shoulder to see if there really was a chest of drawers.

"Do you like to kiss?" she asked, lowering her eyelashes.

"I guess so." I was getting more nervous. "Look, I'm gonna be fired if I don't get back. Mr. Evans is probably out looking for me."

"You kiss dry or French?" she asked.

I had never heard such words. They sounded a little vulgar.

"I just kiss, that's all I do. I just kiss."

"Do you kiss girls the way you kiss your mama?" She tugged playfully at my shirt sleeve.

"Yeah, I guess so," I said. "What's wrong with that?"

"That's the way little boys and little girls kiss," she said scornfully. "Why, you are all grown up now. You need to kiss like adults kiss."

"Whatta you mean, the way adults kiss?"

"Adults French kiss. Kids dry kiss." She kept moving closer every time she said *kiss*.

I made another mistake. I asked, "What's the difference?"

"Come here, I'll show you," she said closing the small gap between us. Feeling her so close was almost overwhelming. I turned and looked toward the stairs hoping her mama would come in.

"Look, don't you think you need to get back downstairs? I know I need to get back to the store."

"Look, Wales," she was getting impatient. "You are grown up. You are a man."

Regardless of the time, I liked to hear what she said, so I turned around and found her right in front of me.

"So," she smiled, "take a minute and I'll teach you how grown-ups kiss. How do you kiss? Show me."

"You mean now? Here in your house?"

"Yes," she said, looking at me as if she'd like to eat me up.

I leaned over and my lips touched hers.

"That's not the way to kiss, Wales. Let me show you."

She put her hands on my jaws and mashed my mouth open.

"Now leave them just like that," she said. "I'll do my lips the same way."

I stood there with my mouth half opened and my cheeks pushed in. She moved real close and whispered, "Close your eyes."

I knew at that moment my life was about to change. I was being introduced into the adult world.

That night I asked Mama if she had ever heard of French kissing.

She said it wasn't nice and to stay away from girls who do.

"Believe me, Mama, I will."

A few days later James and I were walking home from school. He said, "Let's stop in at the Friendly Cafe and get something to drink."

"Naw, not me," I said. "I'm not thirsty."

"OK," James said. "I'll see you later."

As he turned to go in, I called to him, "If the girl behind the counter wants you to move a chest of drawers, tell her you have a hurt back."

"What's wrong with moving a chest of drawers?" he asked.

"It's a man's job, and you're still a boy."

13
Cramming For Chemistry

✤

In the middle of my junior year, school suddenly got exciting. One warm fall afternoon when I didn't think I could stay awake till English class was over, a big, tall fellow walked into our classroom. Now I was tall, six feet five, but this "student" (I use the term loosely) was even taller. I could tell he was no country bumpkin by the way he dressed. He was big time.

Mrs. McKinney seated him next to me. It didn't take me long to learn he came from a town in Alabama where he had so many problems the school expelled him. His mama and daddy had relatives in Tallapoosa, so he was sent there to finish school. When he told me his problems, I knew we were two peas in a pod.

Cooter and I were inseparable. We double-dated, drank, joined in kid-stuff gambling, paid no attention in classes, and joined in the fun of putting tacks in Mrs. McKinney's chair. No matter how many times we did it, she never looked in her chair before she sat down. We doubled over laughing when she walked down the hall rubbing her back end. When she turned around and glared, we started turning the combination on our lockers. She suspected it was us but never could catch us.

Cooter was the best-dressed boy in school. He wore an English tweed jacket with suede elbow patches, twin flaps on the pockets, and a belt on the back. If I had asked to borrow it, I might as well have asked for his life. His clothes came first.

The uncle he lived with ran one of the pool rooms and let us play on the back table when there were no customers. He could play "9 Ball" better than any man or boy in town. He was on his way to being a real pool shark. When he played pool, he took off that tweed jacket. When I wanted to beat him I'd pick it up and put it on. He always glared at me.

"It's OK, Cooter." I assured him I wouldn't hurt it. He couldn't play his best pool as long as I had on his coat.

We never had money for milk shakes at the soda fountain in Dr. Waldrup's drug store. But when Cooter enticed some unsuspecting pool player into a game of "9 Ball," we'd end up with money for a thick chocolate shake with a little malt in it.

Life moved into high gear when we were seniors. Cooter and I took our dates to the junior-senior prom, laughed when our teacher had trouble fitting us for caps and gowns, and planned what we would do in the spring when our whole class went to the Gulf for our "class trip." But even these important events paled by comparison when we thought about getting our class rings.

Why I went to Daddy for the $18.75 for the ring, I don't know. He had never given me even a nickel. Now he gave me his knuckles with a growl. "Graduation is nothing but a bunch of humbug! I've told you many times you should just quit school!" In the past when he had said this, Mama would get furious and let us both know that as long as she was living, there would be no quitting school. We both knew that was the final word on the subject. Now I was getting close to her goal for me.

I walked away from Daddy totally dejected. I knew we were poor, but not that poor. I wandered through the house and found Mama in the kitchen. When I told her what Daddy had said, she didn't say anything. I saw her shoulders drop and heard her sigh as she turned and looked sadly at me.

The next day at school the salesman from Balfour took everybody's ring size. The boys' rings would have a black onyx stone with the school's initials on top. Our name and the year were engraved inside. That ring was as important to me as those won by boys who play in the Super Bowl. It would make me feel important, like a school football letter on a sweater. It showed I had accomplished something. I'd feel a real sense of pride wearing it.

My teacher called my name to come forward and be fitted. I walked up to her desk like I had the money in my pocket. I even said to the salesman, "Hope it won't be long."

71

"About two weeks," he said and told my teacher the size to write by my name.

My heart was heavy when I got home from school. I didn't understand why Mama told me to go to a certain home, pick up the family's laundry, and bring it to our house. Next morning, she asked me to make a fire under the big wash pots and fill them with water. This became my everyday chore.

Cooking three meals a day, keeping the house spotless, washing neighbors' laundry and ours meant Mama never stopped. She even ironed clothes late into the night.

Seaborn and I delivered the big baskets full of starched and ironed clothes. Mama's laundering was better than any cleaners could do today. It made me mad when some folks wouldn't pay us when we delivered their clean clothes. Instead, they loaded us down with vegetables from their gardens, homemade jellies, preserves, or syrup. We complained to Mama, but she'd just say, "Put it in the kitchen."

I didn't think much about how hard she worked. When I did question her, she would say, "Just trying to keep bones together." But she never stopped.

I was worried, for "Ring Day" at school was coming, and I had no idea how I would pay for mine. Excitement mounted as the day drew nearer. My class was jubilant when the announcement came for all seniors to pick up their rings. Outwardly I acted as happy as all the others, but inwardly I died.

What would I do? What could I say? There were kids as poor as I, and some worse off. They were all getting rings. My hands began to sweat, and I felt my shirt sticking to my back. To stave off total embarrassment, I slipped up to my teacher and told her I had lost my money.

"That's all right, Wales. We will hold your ring and you can bring the money tomorrow."

I was off the hook for the moment. I went back to my seat and began cutting up like everything was fine. Maybe I would die and not ever have to pick up my ring.

The next morning at breakfast I said, "This sure is good oatmeal, Mama."

"I bet I've cooked a 100 bushels of oats for you boys," she said and passed the hot biscuits to me.

"As long as Miss Pet keeps giving us this good butter, I bet I could eat a pan full of these," I said, and lathered them with butter and hot sorghum syrup.

"Eat up, boys. It'll put meat on your bones."

"Mama, everybody got their rings yesterday," I said, and sopped up the last of the sorghum. She looked helpless and hurt. She reached across the table and patted my arm. I got up to leave for school, and she stood up and kissed my cheek. Nothing more was said.

All the rings were the same, but my schoolmates examined each others like they were rare jewels. I got tired of telling different stories about why I didn't have mine. My best excuse was it was sent back because it was too tight. That satisfied my friends, but I dreaded the day when even that excuse would run dry. I did confide in Cooter about not having any money for my ring. He didn't have any I could borrow.

One evening Mama stopped washing and ironing. She came out on the porch and sat in the swing between me and Seaborn. I asked her why she was not working like usual. She didn't say a word, just reached into her apron pocket, pulled a box out, and gave it to me.

"What is it?"

"Open it," she said.

My heart jumped from my breast to my throat. It was my class ring. To this day I'm still a "Mama's boy."

Chemistry was required to graduate so in our last semester, Cooter and I couldn't put it off any longer. Our teacher, who was also the principal, announced that most of the class was exempt from the final exam. He said only four students had to take the test. Cooter, two girls and I were asked to remain for a few minutes after class. He told us there would be 100 questions—50 true or false and 50 multiple choices. He even gave us the chapters in the book these questions were taken from and encouraged us by saying, "I want to see you young people graduate. That's why I have made the assignment so easy. Even so, I'm afraid some of you still won't pass; you simply won't apply yourselves." He looked directly at Cooter and me. "If you do fail, you'll be back next year."

The threat of not graduating sent cold chills up and down my spine. "Be back next year" rang louder in my head than the school bell.

Consternation etched both our faces when Cooter and I walked out of the classroom. We stopped at the water cooler in the hall. Whiskey would have helped more, but we had to settle for water.

Cooter looked at me and, in desperation, asked, "What are we going to do, Wales?"

I just shook my head. I had no idea. We had two days to study before doomsday.

That night, I opened the textbook, looked over the ten chapters, and, feeling totally helpless, closed it. "The chickens come home to roost" was Mama's saying I now understood perfectly. Between what I knew and what Cooter knew, an F would have looked good.

I knew it wasn't Providence since we were not yet acquainted, but the next day my civics teacher sent me to the office to get some blue books for our test. I loved civics, history, and geography and made good grades in those subjects. When I picked up the blue books, lo and behold, the teacher's pet was typing in the corner of the office. I asked what he was doing.

"This is the stencil for the chemistry test," he said with a note of importance.

I got so excited, I thought I'd faint. "Let me see it."

"This is the test for your class!" He covered the page with his hands. "You can't look at it!"

I grabbed him by the arm and escorted him down the stairs into the basement. After our "conversation" in which I swore I'd break his fingers so he would never type again, he agreed he would leave the stencil in the typewriter until the next morning. He could tell the teacher the bell rang before he had time to run off the test on the duplicator.

I was so nervous I thought I might even fail the civics test. When I finished, I ran all the way to the pool room to find Cooter. I told him about the stencil.

"Let's go," he said.

Everyone had left the school building except the janitor. He always cleaned the office last before locking the door. When he finished, he saw me and Cooter hanging around in the hall. "What you boys doing here this time of day?" He was suspicious of our motives.

"I lost my pencil and believe I left it in the office. Could I go in and look for it?"

"Guess so, but hurry. I'm fixing to close up."

A steel outside window in the office had a hand lock. With my heart beating a thousand beats a minute, I unlocked it. Cooter and I walked out and told the janitor, "I found my pencil. Do you want me to lock the door?"

"Yes, I will walk out with you boys and lock the front door," he said.

We emerged into the sunlight from the quiet school and waved good-by to the janitor. When we rounded the edge of the building, we started jumping and shouting, "Victory!" We made our plans as we walked down the sidewalk. "Midnight," we agreed as we parted ways.

The streets were quiet as I made my way to our meeting point. I felt like a spy on a mission. Cooter was leaning against the streetlight, inhaling deeply his hand-rolled cigarette.

"You been waitin' long?"

He dropped his cigarette and ground it out with the toe of his shoe. "Naw, just long enough to take a smoke. Let's get going."

We kept our eyes peeled for any witnesses. Cooter leaned against the building to keep watch as I reached up and pulled at the bottom of the window. "Oh, no! The janitor must have locked it back." I looked desperately at Cooter. He reached up and gave it a shove. It pushed open easily. "Ha," I said, "I had you for a minute." He gave me a sarcastic smile before we scrambled up the wall and squeezed through the window. It was dark in the office, but the street light shone pale through the window and gave us just enough light to make our way through the room. There it was, still in the typewriter with all 100 questions.

I carefully extracted the stencil and held it up to the window and read the questions while Cooter wrote them down. We replaced the stencil in the typewriter, crawled out the window, and headed for the first street light. We read some of the questions, and our elation dropped to zero. We just looked at each other. We had no clue what the answers were.

It was 1:00 AM. The test was at 8:00. How would we ever learn enough to pass in seven hours? We stood in the pool of light totally despondent. "Hey, I know what we can do," Cooter looked at me with a gleam in his eye. "You remember my cousin, Annie Mae, who graduated two years ago? Her best subject was chemistry. Let's go get her to help us."

Because Cooter was kinfolk, Annie Mae's mama let her come to the door. "What in the world do you boys want at this hour," she said yawning. We explained our problem. She giggled and pushed the door open. "Come on in and let me look at those questions." She led us into the dining room. We sat around the table and held our breath while she silently read over the questions. At the end of the page, she looked up at us seriously and said, "Why, these are easy." We both let out our breath at the same time.

By 3:00 AM Annie Mae had filled a page with all the answers. My happiness turned to near panic when Cooter reminded me we could only bring to class our #2 pencil.

"We can't take this pad of answers with us," I moaned. Then I thought of Paul. "I bet Paul could shoot the answers with his camera and make a picture small enough to fit in our palm."

Around 4:30, we were at Paul's house. His mama and daddy had made him a room in the basement. He used to slip out at night, and they never knew it. We knocked on his window till he finally woke up and let us in. When I showed him what we wanted, he said the right words, "This is easy."

By 6:00—mission accomplished!

When we walked into the classroom we were given a blue book. We had our pencils. Our teacher sat in the middle of the room and assigned the four corners to us.

I wiped my palms on my pants legs before I wrote my name on the blue book. The teacher said, "Keep everything off your desk except your book and pencil. There will be no looking around. You'll have exactly one hour. Good luck."

We were smart enough to agree Cooter would miss questions at the end of the test and I'd miss some near the beginning.

I had all my answers in five minutes, but leaned my head on my hand, shifted in my seat, rattled my papers, and sat there squirming like it was the hardest test I'd ever taken. Finally, one girl got up and handed in her blue book. A few minutes later Cooter did the same, then me. We left the other girl struggling for the answers.

The next day my homeroom teacher told me to report to the principal's office. When I walked in Cooter was sitting in the outer office.

"What's wrong?" I asked, sitting down beside him. "Do you think they know?"

"I don't know, but you'd think as hard as we worked, they'd let us graduate."

The principal came to the door and asked us in. He motioned to the two chairs facing his desk. We sat down easy like and watched as he picked up our test books. He didn't say a word—just looked them over and smiled. "You boys amaze me," he said.

"How?" I asked, afraid to smile yet.

"Do you know both of you made 87? That's a B+! Have you boys ever made a B+ before?"

Cooter said, "No, sir."

"I did once in spelling."

"I went over your books several times since you both made an 87. You couldn't have cheated because you missed different questions." He stood up and shook our hands, told us how proud he was of us. "It just proves you can do as well as anybody if you apply yourselves."

"Yes, sir," I said. "I never worked so hard in all my life. I stayed up all night before the test."

"Aren't you proud?" he asked.

"Just proud as can be," I replied, now smiling from ear to ear.

It took me years to learn I could accomplish much more by putting my energies in studying rather than cheating.

I lost contact with Cooter after graduation and didn't see him for many years. Would you believe I preached his funeral?

14
Fleeing Regimentation

Basketball was my game in high school. Since I was so tall, I played center. Our team was so good Joe Weathers and I were invited by the basketball coach at Georgia Tech to visit the campus. We were thrilled, for everything was perfect in our eyes regarding Georgia Tech.

Joe, Googie, James, and I had watched Tech play football at Grant Field in Atlanta. James owned an old car that wasn't the kind most people would be proud of, but we were. When we'd go to the games, we covered it with black and gold crepe paper, which were Tech's colors. When you saw us, you knew "country" was coming to town. But who cared? I know we didn't.

The tradition at Georgia Tech is for the cheerleaders to enter the stadium in a Model A Ford painted gold and black. The football team follows, and all the fans start cheering. The games were so exciting I hardly sat down.

Joe and I were elated to be recruited for the basketball team. Googie, who was Joe's cousin, drove us to Atlanta on our promise to get him in the game free.

It was in the fall of 1946 when we arrived on the Georgia Tech campus at 3:00 P.M. We went to the coach's office. He showed us around the gym and locker rooms, gave us three passes to the game, and told us to meet back at the gym by 6:00.

Googie sat in the stands, but Joe and I sat on the bench with the team. The gym was packed. Tech was playing Kentucky, coached by Adolph Rupp. That night U.K. didn't let up on Tech. Both teams were fast. They were constantly running, always running. My heart sank with every Kentucky goal.

Fleeing Regimentation

During a time-out, I looked at Joe and asked, "Whatcha think?"

"This ain't our league," he responded.

"You're right," I said.

At halftime, I looked up in the stands and caught Googie's eye. I motioned to him, "Let's go."

We didn't want to face the coach afterwards. First, he was going to lose badly, and second, we had wasted his time.

Heading home, we knew it was an honor to sit on the bench with coaches and players from Georgia Tech. Nobody from Tallapoosa had ever done that.

I received a call from the North Georgia College basketball coach asking me to visit the campus. I rode the Greyhound. It was the fall of the year, and the mountains in North Georgia are near the southern terminus of the Appalachian Trail. To a flatlander like me, they were spectacular. I wished Mama could see those gold and red tree-covered mountains. She would say, "They are a sight for sore eyes."

I knew I would feel right at home because this county was better known for bootlegging than mine. I could see why. The whiskey-makers could sure hide in these mountains.

The college was in the little town of Dahlonega, a Cherokee Indian word that meant precious yellow metal. It was the site of the first American gold rush in 1828. The college didn't have an athletic dormitory, so I stayed in the men's dorm right on the square of the town. It was an old building. Not nearly as old as my house, but it had indoor commodes which pleased me.

The college was a military school. I walked around campus in the afternoon and saw all the boys dressed like West Pointers. I was impressed, but I didn't want to wear a uniform in college.

I stayed in a room with three other boys. We were sitting around having fun talking when a student opened the door and shouted, "Lights out in ten minutes."

"Can you believe that?" I said to my roommates. "It's only 9:50!"

"If these lights are not off in ten minutes, you'll have a work detail. And, boy, you ain't never seen a work detail like they have here. Good

79

night," he said, and crawled in the lower bunk.

I climbed in the top bunk and thought about the uniforms, discipline, and soldier-boy stuff for a long time. In my heart I knew this place and me would never get along. So, like at Tech, I planned to get up next morning and quietly leave.

Sometime after midnight, and way before daylight, I heard this crazy whistle in the hall. Someone beat on a bucket, the lights went on, and I opened my eyes to see my bunk buddies up putting on their clothes. "What's wrong?" I asked, wondering what on earth had happened.

"Time to get up," they replied, like this was the normal time to rise.

I looked at the clock on the desk, rubbed my eyes and looked again. It was only 4:45 A.M.

"Not for me. I'm going home," I said, and pulled the cover up and rolled over. I felt a stick poking in my back. I turned over and there stood a kid who didn't look 14. I wondered how anyone got up and dressed this early. I understood part of the reason when I noticed he didn't even shave.

"Get out of my room, or I'll throw you out!" I said in my deepest bass voice.

He clicked his heels and left, only to return in a few minutes with several other boys. This time the Hairless Wonder ordered me to get out of bed.

"I'm a guest here. I'm no soldier. Turn out them lights and leave me alone."

The whole bunk was turned over and those little cadets were all over me. I pushed two off, but the whole bunch pushed me into the hall. All four grabbed me, and in the next second, we were tumbling down a flight of stairs. When we hit bottom, we came face to face with the commanding officer. The cadets saluted and were dismissed. I was commanded to report to the coach's office.

I got on the bus instead. As I rode out of Dahlonega, I thought, "If the people here had been as nice as the scenery, I would have liked it fine."

15
The Cotton Mill

Like all long-anticipated events, graduation didn't give me the lasting happiness I expected. I was happy to be finished with school but sad to leave friends. Families didn't move much back then, so I graduated with people I started with in first grade.

The first time I fell in love was in first grade, and when we all turned our caps and gowns in, there she stood. I told her, "It all started with you. Can I have a kiss?"

"I don't see why it would make any difference. The first one didn't," she said and gave me a big smack. That hurt my ego, but, oh well, this was graduation, and I couldn't let her spoil the day.

As soon as the graduation fun wore off, I was drafted. Upon my discharge from the Navy two years later, I was aware more than ever of the emptiness of my life. A steady job that paid more than the Navy or taxi-driving would fill one pressing need. There weren't many places to find a job except the cotton mill. Buck Barnes was the boss and happened to be Mama's good friend. I went to his office to ask him to hire me.

Mr. Barnes' secretary was typing and looked up, surprised to see me. "Just take a seat there by the water cooler, Wales. Mr. Barnes is out in the mill and will be right back."

I eased my big frame down on one of those old wooden office chairs and looked around at the dusty place. Lint had even seeped into the office. Buck Barnes walked in and stuck out his hand like he was glad to see me. He was handsome and stood almost at eye level with me. "How's your mama doing, Wales?"

"Fine. She's just fine," I said.

"You got a good mama. Not many like her. She thinks a lot of you boys. Now, what can I do for you?"

"I need a job."

"What kind of job?"

"Whatever you've got."

"Why, I thought you were going off to college to get an education. Don't you want to play ball? Wales, think a long time before you decide to spend your life in a cotton mill. This work is hard, the pay poor, and there are not many opportunities to advance. No, you don't want to be tied down to cotton-mill work," Buck said, looking at me searching my motives.

"I'm not afraid of hard work. I need a chance."

"Does your Mama know you're down here?" he asked, knowing she would not approve.

"No, sir." I squirmed in my chair.

"What do you think she would say about you working here?" he asked.

"I don't know," I said, but I did. She would not approve.

"Well," he said, and leaned over his desk toward me to make his point, "I do! And I don't believe she has poured her life into you boys the way she has to have you end up in this cotton mill."

"Will you let me try?"

He pushed back his chair, stood up, and walked over to the dirty window. He stood there for a few minutes, looking down at the mill yard. I didn't know what he was thinking. Finally he broke the silence, "Come over here, Wales, and take a good look. You see those people down there?" It was shift-change time, and I saw workers leaving the mill covered with lint.

"Some of them have been here all their lives, as their families before them. They're good people. They work hard and never complain. You know what they get for wages? They pay the company weekly rent for the house they live in. They can buy only the necessities of groceries, maybe a licorice stick for their youngest, Bull Durham tobacco for the father, and a can of snuff for his wife. He may have picture-show money for Saturday night if he doesn't have many doctor bills to pay. He doesn't carry a billfold, just a change purse. His wife will carry what little she gets tied up in a handkerchief. Is this your ambition?"

I was sure it couldn't be that bad, so I said I'd like a try.

"All right, be here at 11:45 tonight. I'll start you on the third shift."

My heart sank when he mentioned the night shift, but I answered, "Yes, sir."

"When you report to work, don't dress in your school clothes. Wear what you want to throw away."

I was hired! I didn't tell Mama I was going to work that night. I just went.

At 11:30, I joined a group of mill workers who were standing around waiting for the whistle to sound work time. The men had on baggy overalls with plaid shirts, brogans, and wool socks. Folks that I knew spoke to me. Some asked what I was doing there.

"Going to work," I said with a hearty handshake and smile as if this was the best shift to work.

"Why, boy, you won't last a week in this mill. Who was fool enough to hire you?" a mill veteran asked.

The men laughed, the women giggled. I noticed a lot did not wear their false teeth. Maybe they didn't have any or couldn't afford them.

The whistle blew. A foreman met me at the big door. The machines were so noisy he just motioned me to follow. We walked up to the second floor, and he gave me a broom and assigned a specific area to keep clean. Lint, coming out of those machines, flew everywhere. Some workers wore a handkerchief over their mouth and nose. I started sweeping. When I got one spot clean, the one I had just finished had inches of lint. Somebody was always yelling at me, "Get that broom over here. Do you want my machine to stop?"

After a few hours, the whistle blew for a break time. The big machines stopped, and everybody headed for a window or outside. The heat was withering, and there was no air-conditioning. I went out to a loading platform where fifteen or twenty men stood. The cool night air revived me.

The men all used tobacco. They either chewed, dipped, or smoked.

There was a lot of conversation, but when a woman passed, they would all punch each other. One chubby woman walked by who was rather homely looking to me. A fellow punched me and said, "How about that?"

"Yeah," I said, "she's something." I wondered why they got excited over a plain woman like her. Then I remembered they went to work at 11:30 and got off at 8:00 A.M. After breakfast, they just fell in bed and stayed there till late in the afternoon. They just didn't have an opportunity to go out. Maybe that was the reason this woman looked so good to them.

The whistle sounded again, reminding me of the ones I was used to at basketball games. Everybody went back to work. I had been there only three hours and already felt blisters coming on my hands from the broom. I picked it up and started sweeping again. The machines roared, and the lint flew in clouds. A foreman yelled at me, "Goebel! Get over here. If this machine stops because of your laziness, you will be the one to pay."

My laziness! My arms were so tired, I thought they'd fall off. I can't think of many things that ever made me as happy as hearing the 8:00 A.M. whistle. I was totally wiped out.

One fellow walked over and put his sweaty arm on my shoulder. He said, "You did pretty good for a city slicker."

"A city slicker?" I never thought living in Tallapoosa qualified me for that title. But town boys lived on one side of the tracks and cotton mill boys on the other.

"Get some rest, boy. You gotta do better tonight," the foreman ordered.

That did it. I walked outside. Lint covered my clothes, my hair, and filled my nose, ears, pockets, and shoes. I brushed till I finally got most of it off, then walked back into Buck's office. His secretary asked me to have a seat. I sat in the same old wooden chair as the day before. In a few minutes, Buck came in. "Come on in," he said, and walked on into his private office. He looked at me and asked without a trace of surprise, "You're quitting?"

"Yes, sir."

"Sit down," he said. "Now, boy, if you want anything better than this, you'd better make up your mind to go on to college."

I asked if the mill would pay me for my eight hours of work. He reached in his pocket and pulled out a ten-dollar bill. "I didn't put you on the mill payroll. I didn't think you would last. But, it's better this way; now you see the need for college. And by the way, if the mill had paid you, it wouldn't have been that much."

As I started out the door, Buck said, "Wales, you come and see me and my wife this Saturday. You hear?"

"Yes," I said, "and thanks for this." I walked out holding my ten-dollar bill.

I couldn't imagine why the Barneses wanted me to come see them. Guess curiosity took me Saturday afternoon to their door. Mrs. Barnes invited me in. She and Buck had a beautiful home full of antiques. Her new furniture blended in with the old things and made them more outstanding. She was one of the prettiest ladies I'd ever seen. There wasn't a woman sweeter, unless it was Mama. Her maiden name was Crawford. The Crawfords gave more to Tallapoosa than money can buy. They gave the town class. You find folks like them in every small town in the South.

Buck was reading the paper on the back patio. He stood up, shook my hand, and asked me to take a seat.

"You thought any more about college?" Buck asked and laid his paper on the glass-top table.

"Well, yes. You were right about the cotton mill. I don't want to spend my life working there," I replied.

Buck said he had gotten in touch with two of my old high school friends who were attending West Georgia College in Carrollton. They had agreed to meet Buck and me the next day, Sunday, in front of the administration building on campus. He asked if I'd go.

"Sure," I said.

I really must say that I have no logical answer as to why the Barneses were concerned for my education. I met the Barneses after lunch at

Smith's Cafe, crawled in the back seat of their car, and thought to myself, "What am I doing?"

Carrollton was 25 miles from Tallapoosa. All the way Mrs. Barnes kept assuring me how much I would enjoy college. I had a world of confidence in Mrs. Barnes, so I said, "Yes, ma'am."

My friends were waiting, and the five of us sat on the front steps discussing the school. They all told me how much I would like it. I appreciated all this concern but asked Buck if I could take a walk for a few minutes with my buddies. "Tell you what," Buck said, "we'll go for a drive and pick you up in an hour."

"Great," I said.

When they drove off, one of my friends said, "Wales, man, this place is where you want to be. Girls are everywhere, and we party all the time, even in our dorm. We have some older married students as house parents, but they don't pay any attention. It's great."

"I want to play basketball." I asked, "Can I make the team?"

One replied, "Guarantee you will."

Buck said, as we drove back to Tallapoosa, "Well, what do you think?"

"You've convinced me. I'm going to college. Looking forward to hitting the books again." This was a lie because the thing that convinced me was my talk with the guys about girls, parties, and basketball.

"Good," said Mrs. Barnes, proud as if I were her own.

16
Proctor

✣

Collwhere have you been all my life? If college was for anybody, it was for me. Everything my buddies predicted that fateful day the Barneses drove me over to see the campus was fulfilled and then some. It was girls, parties, and basketball. I not only made the team, but I also played my favorite position, center. Playing ball was my idea of what college ought to be.

It's a known fact that all girls from Georgia are pretty. That's why we refer to them as "Georgia peaches." The guy who wrote "Georgia on My Mind" wasn't thinking of home cooking; he was thinking of those "peaches." I had my pick. I was like a boy turned loose in a candy store with the owner gone. This was real living.

It didn't take me long to identify two kinds of students on campus. One kind actually worked for a degree. The other lived life like one big party.

I remember the smell of the Greyhound's diesel pouring from the back of the bus in a black cloud as it left me in Carrollton. It was a short walk to the campus that sat on a little hill. I took a deep breath to calm my nerves, for I wanted to appear confident when I met my roommates. Four large old brick buildings faced a semicircle drive. The administration building where the Barneses and I met my buddies was the largest, but the library at the back of the circle was newer and nicer.

My dorm, Rogers Hall, wasn't on the circle, but back behind the big buildings. I never understood how they could call a discarded military barracks from World War II a "hall." It housed sixteen boys. I dropped my bag in the lobby and surveyed the list posted with room assignments. Out by my name was the word *proctor*. What in the world was a proctor?

All the boys were moving in and stopping to find their room assignments. I didn't want them to know I was so ignorant that I didn't know what *proctor* meant. A Webster's Dictionary lay on a nearby table. I looked up the word and did a double take. It really said, "proctor—supervisor of students." Me, a proctor? It must be a mistake.

Dumfounded, I was still staring at the dictionary when Dean Roberts, dean of students, came in. He introduced himself, explained my responsibilities, told me he knew I'd do a great job, and assured me if he could help in any way his door was always open. His open door would prove true, but not the way he intended. He suggested I call the boys together and let everyone introduce themselves. "Let it be democratic," he said (*democracy* was the "in" word after WWII). "Work together to make each man feel part of the family."

When he left, I did exactly as he said. We all met in the lobby. What a group. There was a fellow from La Fayette who ended up playing cards day and night. Another was from Athens. He later committed suicide. A boy from outside Buchanan fell and broke his neck his junior year. And when you have a group like these fellows, there will be one who will steal anything not tied down. We had ours. If we had a scholar, I never knew it.

After we introduced ourselves, I asked if anyone had anything to say. The boy who would eventually commit suicide said, "Yes, let's adjourn to the VFW."

Cheers went up all around. The Veterans of Foreign Wars Club was open to everyone—even to fellows who had not been in the service.

I crawled into Baker's car. He was handsome and had a mustache like Clark Gable. He asked me, "Where did you say you're from, Goebel?"

"Tallapoosa."

"I understand they make great moonshine in that part of Georgia. You ever drink any of it?" he asked.

"A little," I said, and smiled.

"Are you the proctor?" he asked.

"Yeah," I replied. I was glad I knew what I was.

"You'll do just fine as proctor," he said.
I said, "I'll do my best to be democratic."

17
The Banker's Daughter

✣

Early in my freshman year, my date for the first college dance was the prettiest "peach" on campus. I fell in love with her like all the others before, and to beat all, her daddy was the president of a small bank in Georgia. She was the only girl in college with a mink stole.

Baker filled me in on what is expected at a college dance, so I was prepared when I picked up Sarah. I was dashing in my black tuxedo, and she looked like Scarlett O'Hara in her blue off-the-shoulder evening gown. It had yards of material in the skirt and made a swishing sound as she walked down the double staircase toward me. I wasn't sure how to pin my corsage to her dress. There was too much bare skin and not enough dress. She said, "Let me do it," and pinned it to the little bit of cloth on her shoulder.

Hand in hand, we strolled across the lawn to the college gym. It was a romantic setting walking under the old oak trees that spread their limbs over the freshly cut lawn. The music from the live band drifted throughout the campus drawing everyone to the dance. The decorating committee had transformed the gym into a wonderland. A glittering mirrored ball was suspended over the dance floor showering flecks of light all around.

"Young Love" was the first song we danced to, and all the beautiful dresses looked as if the days of "Gone With the Wind" had returned to Georgia.

I was impressed because we had a live band rather than the juke box we danced to in high school. But the music included the same melodies of Tommy and Jimmy Dorsey. In high school we just wore dark suits to the proms. Here the fellows' tuxedos accented the girls' long dresses.

"Swing and sway with Sammy Kaye," the band's motto, was exactly how we danced.

Once I drove over to Sarah's hometown to meet her parents. They invited me to have Sunday lunch at the Carrollton Country Club the next weekend. I bragged about it all week to my dorm mates.

Sarah's folks drove onto campus in a big black Cadillac and picked us up at her dorm. I sat in the front seat with her daddy, and my girl rode in the back with her mama. I waved to my buddies as we drove off campus. Leaning out the window, I hollered, "We're going to the country club for lunch!" I wanted everybody to see us 'cause I'd never eaten at a private club or ridden in a Cadillac.

After lunch Sarah and her mama excused themselves to the powder room. Her daddy eyed me and reminded me Sarah was his only child. He couldn't and wouldn't tolerate anybody ever hurting her and asked me if I understood.

"Yes, sir, I sure do," I replied.

He seemed satisfied my intentions were honorable and changed the subject. "Wales, do you like to hunt?"

"Yes, sir," I replied, feeling we were on safer ground.

"You ever hunt duck or quail?" he asked, warming to the subject.

"No, sir, just blue jays."

"How about deer?"

"No, sir, but lots of possum."

"Who do you hunt with?" he asked, looking a little taken back, but he had to say something.

I told him old Joe and Tater, my brother's black hog-killing friends, who had been taking me hunting since I was a little boy. Then another boy we called "White Trash," because best I knew, he never took a bath.

Her daddy quickly found out I was not in the same class as his daughter. He tried another route.

"Where's your hometown?" he asked.

"Tallapoosa," I said, sensing the distance between him and me.

"They make a lot of moonshine in that part of the country, I hear."

"Yes, sir, I suppose so." I held my breath and feared he would ask if I ever drank any. Luckily he didn't.

At our next dance I asked a friend from Rogers Hall to dance a while with Sarah because I wasn't much of a dancer. He was really excited and couldn't wait to put his hand on the mink stole she wore around her shoulders.

While they danced, I walked over to the refreshment table and picked up a glass of punch made by the "Religious Endeavor." The kids in this group were the finest on campus. Smart, articulate, caring, achievers, but they were far from my world. I never dreamed I would one day, years later, join their set. I tipped the little punch cup up and downed it in one gulp. It didn't do for me what the white whiskey did that I had drunk outside the gym during high school dances.

I sat down next to James in one of the metal chairs that lined the gym walls. He lived in another dormitory, but I knew him from the basketball team. He was no Fred Astaire either.

We sat there watching all the dancers. I sipped my second cup of punch wishing for something stronger. "James," I said, looking at my cup in disgust, "It's a shame this crowd doesn't have better punch."

"What do you mean?" he asked.

"I'd like to have a little white whiskey to spice up my refreshments."

His eyes grew big, and he leaned forward with a smile stretching his face. "What do you mean?" he repeated.

"How'd ya like a pint of good moonshine?"

"Yeah!" he said, "I know I would." He was now on the edge of his chair.

I told him my cousin had a pint in his dorm room that was next to Rogers.

"Come on," I said. He didn't need encouragement. I walked up to the boy dancing with Sarah and asked him to entertain her a little longer till I got back. He was tickled pink to help me out and didn't care how long I was gone. Sarah frowned but didn't say anything.

My cousin Buddy never ran out of moonshine. After a short search of his drawers, we found a bottle behind his socks. We had planned to take only a couple of drinks and then return to the dance, because James also had a date dancing with a friend.

But we drank the whole pint and passed out. When I woke up, I turned toward the window. It was daylight. James was lying on the floor. He had been in a bunk, but when the owner came in, he had rolled James out. I got up slowly and went out in the foyer, flopped down in a chair, and held my head. Through the pain of my hangover, I thought about Sarah. I hoped to goodness she had gotten back to her dorm all right.

A shower and shave cleared my head. James and I headed to breakfast at the cafeteria which was in the lower floor of the gym. While sitting there eating eggs and grits, I spotted Sarah across the room. I walked over to her table to apologize, but she wouldn't speak to me. She left her breakfast and marched out. There I was standing alone with everyone staring.

After my first class, I met her in the hall and asked to talk. She told me in no uncertain terms that I had nothing to say that she'd ever be the least bit interested in and from here on to please leave her alone!

One good thing came out of this relationship. I had "lunch" at the country club and rode in a Cadillac. It was all for the best because I liked to hunt possum and her daddy hunted deer.

And another thing, I would never have made a banker.

18
Rat Week

✥

I didn't know it then, but my life was about to change for the better. Not the big change that would come later, but improvement was on the way. It took awhile, but it was the beginning.

I was elected president of the student body, not because of my intellect or ambition but because everyone knew me. Friends who worked on the campaign were so sure of victory that we went to the VFW. Club to celebrate before the votes were counted. My campaign manager and best friend, Billy, was a real politician. He later became president of the Georgia Teachers' Association and was elected to the Georgia legislature.

I won the election only to find my responsibilities were boring. As student body president, I only represented the students at faculty meetings and presided at the weekly chapel services. The stage was at one end of the gym. I had to sit up there with the main speaker and another student who led the prayer. I was thankful they never asked me to pray. I didn't have one. The "Religious Endeavor" took care of those responsibilities. When I had to meet with visiting parents who were considering sending their kids to the college, I was careful not to tell them what my friends told me when Mr. and Mrs. Barnes took me to see the campus.

I did manage to arrange some perks which made being president bearable. The best was "Rat Week Court."

"Rat Week," when the freshmen were initiated, was a favorite time for me and my buddies. Any freshman caught not abiding by some of the rules of rat week was brought to court. I was the judge and jury and passed judgment; there was no defense, just my verdict.

The basketball team made an agreement with me. If they saw a

94

freshman girl they wanted to date, they would bring her to court, even if no rules had been broken. My sentence would be for her to take the boy to a movie within the next two weeks, pay his way, and buy the popcorn. The girls were too scared to protest. They all submitted, not knowing of our scam.

One afternoon while holding court and passing sentences, Joe, a friend of mine from Rome, Georgia, approached the bench with a girl. She stood behind him as he told all the wrong things she had done. He suggested I throw the book at her. This girl was different. She was the prettiest one I had ever seen. I sat there stunned, staring at this brown-eyed beauty. Joe looked at me funny. I had never before been at a loss for words, but I sat speechless before this girl.

I recovered and said, "Joe, go to the dining room and when you have finished eating come right back. You understand?"

"Yes," Joe said, but the puzzled look on his face showed he didn't.

"Go find another girl, and I'll throw the book at her."

I had decided I wanted this girl for my date.

Joe looked over his shoulder as he left the girl standing alone in front of me. She was dressed for "Rat Week" and looked the worst she'd ever look the rest of her life. Her hair was plaited in 40 pigtails with a little ribbon on each. She had on no lipstick, rouge, or powder. On one foot, she wore a saddle oxford and the other a high-heel shoe. Her skirt was one of those funny broomstick skirts worn upside down and gathered and held up at the waist with a belt. In spite of her "Rat Week" costume, her real deep beauty made my heart jump.

"What's your name?" I asked.

"Jean," she said, not one bit afraid of me.

"Jean who?"

"Jean Duff" was her not-to-be-intimidated answer.

"Jean, why did Joe bring you in?"

"I really don't know."

"Well, there had to be a reason. You broke some rules. I'll have to sentence you. You'll have to take me to the movie instead of Joe," I told her. "How's that?"

"If that's what I've got to do, I guess I will," she responded, not at all impressed that I was the president of the student body or the center on the basketball team.

She didn't help my ego.

A couple of nights later, two of my friends and their freshmen dates, along with Jean and me, went to the only movie theater in Carrollton. We always sat on the back row, and if anyone else was there, we made them move. We upperclassmen were excited about getting our freshmen girls on that row. To my dismay Jean said she wouldn't sit there. She preferred halfway down in the middle of the theater. I asked if she didn't want to sit with the friends we came with?

"Only if they sit in the middle" came her unexpected reply.

I was flabbergasted but followed her down to the middle row. Early in the movie, I put my arm on the back of her seat. She removed it. I waited awhile and tried again. She said, "Please don't put your arm there."

I fumed and kept my arms still but hoped for another chance while walking back to the campus.

Cars were still scarce right after World War II. Only a few students had one. It was about a mile to town. Everybody walked. On our way back, there were two or three places where the trees and shrubs made the street nice and dark. The boys normally began telling their dates good night there. Everybody else was stopping, but Jean kept walking. I asked her what was wrong. "Nothing."

"Why aren't you stopping like the other girls? Are you different? Or do I just turn you off?"

"If stopping and kissing and whatever else you want me to do makes me different, then yes, I'm different. Personally, you don't turn me off. If whatever reason you wanted to go out with me has not fulfilled your expectations, then I'm sorry. But, really, you have nothing to complain about. I paid for your ticket, bought your popcorn, and I have never done that for a boy before."

I walked her to the steps of her dorm where she turned and said politely, "Good night." She marched up the broad steps of Nelson Hall without even a handshake. This was a first for me. I was left standing there with my mouth open, looking at the front door only to see the housemother peering out the little windows. She guarded her girls like an old hen guarding her chicks.

I sat on the broad steps and waited about an hour for my two buddies. Curfew was 10 PM, and they didn't come a minute earlier. As we walked back to Rogers, they were like two colts let out of the barn into the pasture. "How did it go with you, Wales?" asked one.

"A total blowout. I would've died if I'd bought the tickets. I'm writing her off. A whole evening wasted!"

For some strange reason I didn't understand, I couldn't get Jean off my mind. I figured she didn't like me, or maybe she had a special fellow back in her hometown in Summerville. I hated to think I was disliked.

I went up to her dorm one night and asked Miss Howard, her dorm mother, if Jean was in. She checked the register where the girls signed out and said Jean had gone to the library. I knew where it was, but it was one place I didn't frequent. I found Jean researching a paper for her English class and walked her back to the dorm. Before saying good night, I asked her to go to a movie—at my expense. She thought for a minute, then said, "Yes, but let's have an understanding. We sit in the middle of the theater and no stops on the way home."

I strolled back to Rogers, mulling over my feelings about this strange girl, and concluded that I must be crazy. I am about to spend 25 cents for her ticket, 10 cents for popcorn, and not one stop!

I went home that weekend and told Mama about this "different" girl I had met. Really, she was weird. She was nothing like the girls I had dated before. Mama, in her wisdom, simply said, "Why, Wales, you're in love."

"No way," I told Mama. But in my heart, though I didn't want to admit it, I knew something was different.

My whole dating life changed from then on. Jean's and my relationship became a partnership. I was no longer the pursuer and Jean the game. We didn't do just what I wanted but what the two of us could do together. There was no arguing, pouting, or jealousy. She was up front, honest. That helped make me honest, except for my drinking.

I didn't have to lie or play silly games with her as I had with other girls, like she was the only girl for me. For the first time, I was building a long-lasting relationship. I began to develop the characteristics of a husband in that I wanted to protect her.

Who would have ever believed it? The best dating in my life was with Jean. We would walk across campus, sit on her dorm steps, have lunch together in the cafeteria, walk back from Mrs. Campbell's music appreciation class in the evening, and know that was all we were going to do.

I've often wondered since then where the two of us would be today if, on that very first date, Jean had not told me, "We're not sitting in the back row," or "Don't put your arm around me." And there would be "no stops between the picture show and dorm." No kissing. To tell the truth, after that first date, I thought I'd been cheated.

Now after 40 years of marriage, three sons, and four grandchildren, I can say, "Thank you, Jean, for being so honest and pure and different. I wish all girls were just like you."

19
Peanut Butter Crackers

✛

Dean Roberts entered my room with a deeply worried face.
"What's wrong, Dean?" I asked.

"Wales, your mother called my office and asked me to tell you your dad died. I want to tell you how sorry I am to have to deliver this bad news. Of course, you will be excused from classes to go home."

I was surprised but not sad. I thanked the dean, packed a few clothes, and headed for the Carrollton bus station. The destination on the front of the bus read "Detroit," its final stop. There would be so many stops at little towns and gas stations that I couldn't calculate how many days would pass before it got to Detroit. I was glad Tallapoosa was only 30 miles away.

The bus was about empty when it pulled out of the station. The heavy door clanked shut. I walked slowly down the aisle and chose a seat so I'd be alone. Remembering Daddy didn't cause any grief in my heart. One of our neighbors told me that once, before he married Mama, she had seen him beating my twin half brothers nearly to death. I had been on the receiving end of his temper, too.

If Daddy ever had a friend, I never knew it. His being an atheist might have had something to do with it. He was the only real atheist I ever knew. Now he was dead from a heart attack.

The bus rolled into a filling station to pick up some country folks going to town. I was so big, none of them wanted to squeeze into the seat next to me. I was glad, for memories of Daddy kept me occupied. I wondered why he never allowed my friends to come and spend the night with me. Even if they just came to play in our yard, and if Mama wasn't home, he would run them off.

In all my nineteen years he never gave me a cent. Oddly enough, I didn't resent it. Even as a little boy, I knew times were hard during the Depression. What I missed more than money was a dad who showed love. I couldn't remember him ever once showing any affection toward Mama. For me to have wanted it would have been a waste of time.

I was following in his footsteps with my drinking. My older half brothers also drank too much, and those who were married abused their wives. Some of them were already divorced.

The bus stopped next at Bowden Junction. It took forever to get an old lady on board. The bus steps were too high for her short fat legs. The driver pulled, and a younger woman outside pushed. They finally managed to get her in, and she took a seat across from me. I heard her moan out loud, "Lordy, Lordy, I hate thinking about getting off this thing."

She didn't have a suitcase, just an old box tied with strings which she kept on the seat beside her. The driver tried to put it in the catch overhead, but she resisted. I figured all she owned was in that worn box.

As we drove toward Bremen, she opened a tin lunch bucket. Inside were soda crackers and peanut butter. She offered me one, since I was the only person close by. I refused, not because I wasn't hungry, but I figured this was all she had to eat before arriving at her destination. She could be going all the way to Detroit.

The bus made a couple of stops to pick up folks waiting by the side of the road. Forty minutes later, we stopped at Jones Chevrolet Company which served as a bus stop in Bremen. I stood up to stretch, and the old lady asked if I would mind helping her get off.

I asked her, "You going to Bremen?"

"Yeah, I came to spend some time with my dead brother's wife. I live with my daughter in Bowden Junction. She's been real good to look after me, but it's good to get away from her family when I can. It's not good for your children to put you up, but I've got no other place to go. Don't know why God lets old folks live to be a burden on their children."

"Why," I said, "I'll bet your daughter and her husband are glad to have you."

"You're too young to be married, but you'll see." Her wrinkled face drew up into a knowing smile.

It was hard getting her off, but the driver and I managed it. The sister-in-law was there and greeted her warmly. She turned to thank me and said, "Sure wish you'd eat the rest of these crackers."

I thanked her kindly and took them, now that I knew she wasn't going all the way to Detroit.

We rode on toward Waco, making stops at Dryden's Cafe and other roadside pickups before reaching Tallapoosa.

I ate the peanut butter and crackers. They reminded me of grade school recess when I helped Norman eat the lunch his mama fixed.

I thought as I rode along, "What's wrong with me? I have a golden opportunity to make something of myself. Mama sure has tried to help me. She'd say, "The Lord knows I have always done right by you boys." My teachers, coaches, and friends like the Barneses were always there trying to make me see the best and not the worst in me.

Nobody knew me like I knew me. On the outside, I was happy-go-lucky, living life to the fullest; on the inside, I was dying. I wasn't a criminal nor, as some folks say, "sorry." In me was an emptiness that I wished could be satisfied with something besides alcohol. I was beginning to feel tired of life, worn out. Was there anybody who could help me?

The bus driver called out, "Tallapoosa." It sounded good, that word *Tallapoosa*. I was home, and where home was, there would be my Mama.

I walked home and found the house filled with Mama's friends. They all had brought food, and Mama's table was full. I took a plate and loaded it with fried chicken, black-eyed peas, and three kinds of cake.

Daddy's coffin was in the front room, but most of Mama's friends sat on the porch or drank coffee in the kitchen. No one would have come to the house, or to the funeral the next day, if it wasn't for Mama.

I went upstairs and lay across my bed. Thoughts of what I'd really like to tell Daddy flooded my mind. I pictured him sitting on the front porch and me coming up and sitting beside him. Knowing him, we would just sit there in silence. Finally I would say, "Daddy, how're you doing?"

"Oh, for an old man, doing about as well as you could expect," I'd hope he'd reply. "How are you?"

"About the same, I guess," I'd say.

Then there would be more silence. Finally I would say, "Daddy."

"Uh-huh," he'd reply.

"I love you," I'd tell him.

More silence.

"It doesn't matter, Daddy, about the past," I'd tell him. "I still love you."

Silence.

20
Someone Greater

✜

Jean and I were dating frequently, and I was in love just as Mama said. Jean felt the same about me. She asked me several times if I drank.

"Of course not. Why do you keep asking me that?"

"The girls in my dorm tell me you drink a lot."

"Oh, they're just jealous that you have a steady boyfriend."

She wanted to believe me.

The students began preparing for our big dance Valentine's weekend. To our surprise, Jean and I were selected by the student body as "Mr. and Miss Valentine." This was big stuff for Jean. She looked forward to walking with me through a huge crepe-paper valentine and leading the first dance. The pomp that went on at big dances bedazzled everyone, especially freshmen.

"Just call me Mr. Valentine," I said, as I climbed into James' old two-door Pontiac after ball practice. We headed for the VFW Club on Highway 27 to drink a few Millers.

"How in the world did you get selected as 'Mr. Valentine?'" James laughed.

"Just my charm and good looks, I imagine," I said with a laugh.

"More like Jean's charms and good looks as 'Miss Valentine.' You just rode on her coattails," James answered.

"I'll have to agree with you," I replied. "She's really excited about the big dance. I'm looking forward to it, too, but not for the same reason."

"Not for being crowned 'Mr. and Miss Valentine' at the dance?" he raised his brows.

"I'm looking to make some easy money. You interested?"

"How?"

I told him what we both knew. There would be an auditorium full of thirsty kids at the dance. We also knew that only a few boys from around Atlanta would bring their own booze. I had a way to supply the others.

"How?" James asked.

I gave his dashboard an appreciative pat and said, "The mighty Pontiac."

He looked puzzled.

"If you'll drive to Tallapoosa, I know a bootlegger who will sell us a gallon of good whiskey for only $3," I said. "He'll also get us the pint bottles with stoppers. We'll need at least five gallons for the first dance."

James face fell. "I don't know about that, Wales. What if we get caught?"

"There's always a chance," I admitted. "I got caught once, but that was when I was young and stupid. If you'll keep your mouth shut, I know the back roads, and the law don't spend much time out there."

A smile slowly spread across his face. "OK. When do we go?" he asked.

"I have to call and make sure it's all clear. Moonshiners seem to know when the law is staking them out."

I put in my request Saturday afternoon. The bootlegger told me to come Wednesday and where the pick-up spot was.

After basketball practice Wednesday night, we started our trip to Tallapoosa. On the way, I told him all my tales of selling moonshine as a kid. I left out the part when I was thrown in jail. It might have scared him off, and I needed his car.

As we turned onto an unpaved river road, our conversation lulled. After a few minutes, I said, "OK, turn off your lights." We drove about two miles with only the road gravel drumming under the car breaking the silence. The moon was full, so visibility was pretty good. My mouth grew dry and my stomach felt a little queasy. "I've missed this excitement," I said quietly.

"Huh?" James said, glancing my way.

"Oh, nothing," I hadn't meant to speak my thoughts. "Slow down. I think that's him. Flash your lights twice."

Lights from an old red pickup responded.

"You stay in the car. He knows me," I said as we pulled up behind the truck.

No words were spoken. We put the whiskey and bottles in the trunk of James' car and paid our money. He went one way, and we went the other.

My tux jacket had four inside pockets. I placed four pints of moonshine in my jacket and headed to Jean's dorm. This would be her honored night. When I saw her, I knew she would be the most beautiful Miss Valentine since Saint Valentine was given his own holiday. She clutched my arm tightly and talked excitedly on our walk across the lawn to the gym.

The lights sprinkled the dance floor from the mirrored ball suspended from the ceiling. The sparkle in Jean's eyes was as brilliant as that reflected on the dancers. I wanted to make sure nothing spoiled the evening for Jean. She never understood why so many guys touched my shoulder and I'd leave for a few minutes to go outside. It got to be aggravating after our dances were interrupted so many times. When we walked back to the dorm, she wanted to know what was going on. I lied, "Just student body business."

James and I continued to sell whiskey for several more dances. We always bottled it in my room at Rogers. It was nice to have money to wine and dine Jean and blow at the VFW. I never knew who reported me to Dean Roberts.

After one dance, the dean was standing in the lobby of Rogers waiting for me. "Hello, dean, is anything wrong?" I asked, hoping my voice didn't give me away.

"Do you smell anything, Wales?"

"I haven't washed my workout clothes in a while," I lied.

"It smells like a still in here." He wasn't smiling.

Luckily I had gotten rid of all the cans and bottles before going to the dance. The dean walked into my room, looked around, and sniffed the air. "The smell is stronger in here," he said. He turned and looked me squarely in the face. "Do you know anyone in this dorm who's been bringing alcohol on campus?"

"No, sir, none I know of," I lied. All my years of lies made it easy to tell tales without batting an eye, but for some reason I had a hard time looking the dean in the eye.

He asked me to come to his office the next morning and turned to leave. "Get this room cleaned up; it's a disgrace," he called over his shoulder.

Dean Roberts was a wonderful person and fair. I never had a teacher, professor, or dean who did not show real interest in me. It's amazing, as I think back, on how the Barneses, the Harpers, the Crawfords, a widow woman named Miss Blackman, and many others in Tallapoosa, each in their own way, reached out to help me. Most did it, I think, for Mama. They knew how hard she was trying to salvage her three sons.

Next morning, I entered the administration building and walked down the hall to the dean's office. He asked me to sit down. He was tall and distinguished, an ideal person to play a college dean in a movie.

I'll never forget Dean Roberts. We worked closely together, since I was student-body president. He played a part in my life my dad never did, and I respected him more than any other man.

"What are your goals, Wales?" he asked, taking his chair behind his desk.

I was a little ashamed to admit I had none.

"What are you trying to prove?"

I wasn't sure what he was getting at, so I shrugged my shoulders. He then gave me something to think about.

"You will probably waste your life away," he said, with real sadness I could see in his face.

Those words cut me like a knife.

He told me of the years he had been in education and how he considered himself knowledgeable of human nature. "How your life winds up will depend totally on the choices you make," he said. "You are not dumb. I've seen you apply yourself and do very well. You have a way of making people like you as evidenced by your election to the student government. I would like to help you, but before anybody can help, you have to want help and want it badly." He was not trying to flatter me. There was no reason to. Then he added, "There are a lot of things going wrong on campus. From what I hear, you are involved in all of them."

I got up to leave.

"Wales, you have access to my office as president of the student government. This privilege extends only when I am here and the door is unlocked."

"I understand," I answered.

"Someone has been coming in after the building is secured. They have been getting my records and marking off unexcused absences for the students. I believe it's you. I just have not caught you, but I will. Wales, I'll help you if you'll let me."

"Yes, sir," I said. "Thank you."

As I walked down the hall, I saw Eugene. He was a good friend and had a nice little Plymouth coupe. He would one day be a fine preacher.

"Hey, Gene," I called, "can I have the keys to your car?"

"Sure, where you going?" he asked while fishing the keys from his pocket.

"Nowhere. I just want to sit in it and think."

"Are you OK?" he asked with concern, for he could tell I was upset.

"Yeah, I'll give the keys back at ball practice," I said.

I knew where he parked on the main campus. I unlocked the door, got in, and locked it back, and just sat there for a few moments with my hands on the steering wheel staring across campus. The old buildings looked majestic, the landscaping beautiful. I loved the college. It was between classes, and kids were hurrying from one building to the next. Teachers walked a little slower.

Mr. Yates walked by using a long stick with a nail in one end stabbing trash someone carelessly threw on the ground. We always said it was the "day" students. We felt they didn't have the same pride as we. Mr. Yates waved. I sometimes played one-on-one basketball with him.

He was tough.

Everything seemed so perfect and peaceful on campus. I looked at myself in the rear-view mirror. I looked as calm as the scene before me, but I felt sick to my stomach. "What's wrong with you? Yeah, as Dean Roberts said, 'Wales, what are you trying to prove?'" I spoke to my reflection in the mirror. For the first time, I saw myself as I really was. It was awful, absolutely awful. To be honest, I had no answer to the dean's question. The only person in all the world who would understand was Mama. If she had just been there. I was alone, all alone like in the jail cell years before.

I leaned my head on the steering wheel and stared at my knees. Tears streamed from my eyes and dripped off the end of my nose leaving wet circles on my pants. I cupped my head in my hands and cried. Sobs came from the back of my throat and shook my whole body. Grief had never before touched me, but now I felt weighted down with years and years of sorrow. How long I sobbed, I don't know.

Some say a good cry makes you feel better. Perhaps in some cases, it's true, but in my case it wasn't. I still hurt when all my tears were used up.

I skipped practice, got drunk, and Jean heard about it. Of course, I denied it.

Jean thought we should start dating other people.

"No, I don't want to date anyone but you. You are the first girl I have really loved." I was ashamed to beg her but I was desperate. "This is not a good time for this kind of talk. I need you, Jean."

Jean was mature for her 18 years, She was a strong person and had goals. She knew what she wanted to do with her life. She was not seeking a career. Her ambition was to be a good wife and hopefully a mother. She had not come to West Georgia looking for a husband but was being obedient to her mom and dad. It was their desire that she should get a good education.

"Wales, I am afraid for you, and for myself as well," she said.

"What are you saying?" I asked.

"It's true, I do love you, and I know you feel the same for me.

Although you have denied it, I know about your drinking. Too many of your friends have told me. I don't know about your kind of life. There was never a beer in my home. My mother warned me about men who abuse alcohol, how they lie and always promise things will be better. Before I get too deeply involved with a person like that, it's best I break it off."

I was stunned. "Jean, how can you say you love someone one minute and the next just cut it off like throwing a switch?"

"It's not as easy as you think." She wiped away tears that were brimming in her eyes. "It hurts me, too." She took a deep breath and drew herself up straight and tall to look me in the eyes. "I do hurt for you, Wales. I wish you were truly like you are when you're with me. But you're not that way."

"Is that it?" I asked. "All the walks, talks, dances, ball games, trips to your and my home? Sitting under the big old oak tree on campus, trying to sneak a kiss and being afraid someone would see us; now you say to me it's over?"

"You need someone greater than me to help you, Wales."

"Who, if not you or Mama?"

"God!"

21
Plain Old Meanness

✥

ife was all uphill now. I lost interest in everything. I was a miserable president of the student government and lost all the respect I had for sportsmanship in basketball. During practice one day, I intentionally tripped a teammate, causing him to injure a leg. Why I did it, I don't know. I liked the guy and knew he thought well of me.

Mama would have called it a streak of meanness. And that's what it was, just plain old meanness.

The coach called me off the court, chewed me out, and made me sit out the rest of practice. He didn't know it, but he did me a favor. I had a hangover.

I had been drinking moonshine openly and didn't care who saw me, except Mama and Jean.

My team went to Atlanta to play Southern Tech. They were always rough but had a good ball club. When I went up for the tip-off at the start of the game, the other center kneed me in the groin. The cheap shot bent me over in terrible pain. Coach called time-out and told me Tech wanted me to foul out, so don't retaliate.

I had played enough to know it was hard for the ref to see everything under the basket. There were things I could do to hurt a player, yet still not get a foul.

Their center and I kept up a personal battle the whole game. We were well ahead in the final quarter, so dirty tricks were beginning to let up, or so I thought. While guarding Tech's center, who was trying to throw the ball down court, he let it fly smack into my face. It broke two of my front teeth. So as he ran by, I tripped him and jumped on top of him. The whistles blew and the refs sent both teams to their benches to cool off.

Just before the game was over, their center jumped for a rebound. As he was coming down, I knocked his legs from under him. He hit the floor hard on his back and neck.

Someone blindsided me, and the next thing I knew, I was waking up in a hospital room. I found out the referee himself had taken me out with a hard body block. We won the game, but I was the loser.

Monday morning, I was called to report to the coach's office at 10 AM. I was on time but sat outside for 15 minutes waiting. In my heart, I was saying, "Please help me, Coach, don't quit on me, too."

"Come on in, Goebel," he said.

I knew from his tone this conference wasn't going to be friendly.

He reminded me he had coached ball, high school and college, for many years but had never had anyone as disruptive to a program as me. He gave me the same lecture as Dean Roberts.

"What's wrong with you, Wales? What are you trying to prove?" he asked. "Boy, you've got ability."

Before this incident, he had wanted me to play at the University of Georgia, but like everyone else, he was giving up. I asked for a second chance.

"No," he said. "You have had too many second chances. Just turn in your uniform, and remember that it is you who messed up your life. Nobody but you."

I met Bob in the hall. He was a good friend and played ball with me. He asked, "You're going to stay in school, aren't you, Wales?"

"I don't know," I replied, as we walked out the front door. We sat down on the steps. I really didn't know. How could I stay in school? Jean was refusing my calls, and now basketball was over. Everything important to me was gone.

I had never seen Bob drink, but I asked him, "You want to get drunk with me?"

"Naw, I don't fool with whiskey," he replied.

Bob later married his college sweetheart. He lived only a short time after marriage. I wondered why the good die young.

I went over to the dorm next to Roger's to see Buddy, my

half-brother's son. He was like a brother to me. We had grown up together. He had graduated from high school a year ahead of me, but waited around so we could go to college together.

"Hey! Buddy, let's go box," I said after I had told him about my troubles.

"It's a good thing you're not a fighter," Buddy laughed, as I sparred with him in the boxing ring. We had turned an old gym next to Rogers into a boxing ring. Buddy could dance circles around me, even though I was bigger than he.

Boxing was Buddy's love. Every Saturday night, Bremen, Georgia, held professional boxing matches. Buddy entered the 150-175 pound class, and I never saw him lose a fight.

Once a fellow from Columbus, Georgia, came up to fight Buddy. He advertised himself as a classical fighter. Before the evening was over, Buddy had taken all his class.

Buddy and I walked back to Rogers after our workout. It was Friday night, and I was lonely without Jean. Rogers was empty except for the two of us. We didn't have anything to do until Ray walked in with a paper sack under his arm.

"What'cha got, Ray?" I asked.

"A gallon of homemade wine. Do you think it'll be safe in my closet?"

"Nobody here but me and Buddy," I replied. I've often wondered if Ray really believed we wouldn't touch his wine after he left.

Alcohol works on folks in different ways. Some of my friends would get high on moonshine and just go to sleep. It made others want to fight. Buddy was the fighting kind. It didn't matter to him who he fought, including me.

Now wine was not my drink of choice because it always gave me a headache. But if that was all the alcohol available, I'd drink it in a hurry. When the wine was gone, my head ached so bad I lay on the bed trying to sleep. Buddy kept hitting me in the back with his fist. He finally stopped, but not for long. He picked up my desk chair and brought it down hard on top of me. I don't know how I got up.

Somehow I survived all of Buddy's licks, including the chair, but the dorm didn't fair as well. I guess we finally passed out. Around one AM we came to enough to see a totally demolished dorm. I told Buddy we'd better leave before the school found out it was us.

I got on the back of his motorcycle. He revved it up, and the back wheel threw up a cloud of burned rubber as we made a hasty getaway. We flew down the road and missed the very first turn, jumped the curb, and skidded across the grass. The motorcycle fell on top of us. We remained unconscious where we had fallen.

The next morning, some students pushed the motorcycle off us. When I stood up and looked across the campus, I saw students going to breakfast. I reached down and pulled Buddy up by his outstretched hand.

"Come on, let's get some breakfast."

"Where?" he asked,

"In the school cafeteria," I said.

"You mean looking like this?" he asked.

We looked as if we had been riding a freight train for a week. "Yeah, what's the difference? We are finished here anyway."

There was a long line waiting for breakfast to be served. I went to the front of the line. Everyone stared at us. They must have wondered, "How could we have ever elected him president?"

The cafeteria director told me to go clean up and added, "You are disgusting."

Without a plate or napkin, I pulled three or four fried eggs off the serving tray, put them all in my mouth, washed them down with a pint of milk, and walked out.

Just outside the door, Jean stood in the breakfast line. I stopped, hoping she'd speak.

She looked the other way. The pain of rejection hurt worse than the fight and the wreck.

My world was collapsing.

22
I'm Sorry

✢

was daydreaming in my Greek mythology class when the instructor asked me to report to the dean's office. I walked across the old campus admiring the grounds, never dreaming the worst day of my life was about to happen. Mr. Yates and his staff kept the grass and shrubbery clipped like a fine manicure. It was the perfect picture of a small southern college in the heart of Carroll County, Georgia.

Dean Roberts' office in the administration building was small for a man with so many responsibilities. The furniture looked as old as the college. All his book shelves were full, and some books and papers were stacked on the floor. He looked up when I walked in and motioned to me to have a seat.

Smoke from the dean's pipe was sweet-smelling and comforting to me. The office grew warm as I sat waiting for him to finish writing what looked like memos. I admired him and looked upon him as a father figure. If and when I became a father, I would smoke a pipe, too.

We had worked closely together since I became president of the student body. I knew Dean Roberts cared for me as perhaps he did for all the students on campus. We had gotten along well. Now his silence made me restless. My mind raced. Why had he called me out of class? I had not been the student he wished me to be. It seemed I sat there for thirty minutes before he quit writing and looked up.

He struggled with what he wanted to say. "Wales, you know I'm going to expel you from school."

Those words were like a bomb exploding inside me. Yes, I did expect it, but deep down I had hoped to be forgiven.

"You're the first president of the student government this school has ever had to expel," he continued.

A knot filled my throat. The temperature in the room seemed to increase 100 degrees. I mopped my brow and sighed deeply. I was full of shame. I didn't want to cry in front of the man I respected more than any other man in my life. I couldn't reply.

"Do you have anything to say, Wales?"

"I... I'm sorry."

"You will be off campus by 5:00 PM," he told me.

It was then mid-morning.

For what it was worth, I wanted to see Jean before I left. I walked to her dorm and asked her roommate if Jean would see me.

"No," she replied. "Give it a few days. Jean cares for you, but she's deeply hurt, and it'll take her a while to get over it."

"I don't have a few days. I've been expelled. I have to leave today."

Jean's roommate was touched by my pain. She hugged me and kissed my cheek.

"I'm sorry, Wales."

"Yeah, me too," I said and walked away.

All of Rogers was waiting for me. The guys treated me like a hero. Eddie wanted me to go to the VFW Club and buy all the beer I could drink. I thanked them all but said I really had to get on home.

The whole dorm followed me into my room. I put the few clothes I had in my duffel bag, but I didn't pack the jackets I had won playing ball. I carried them on hangers. They were my trophies, all I had to account for my time at West Georgia.

Alford wanted to buy my tux. He was my height and size.

I said, "Naw, you can have it."

He took it, then asked, "What's that smell?"

"Moonshine. If you don't like it, you can have it dry-cleaned."

He answered he'd rather have it like it was.

"It may get you in trouble," I warned.

As I got ready to leave, big, cocky men again became little boys. Some of us shook hands, others even hugged me, especially Eddie. I had introduced him to a life of alcohol that would cause him to commit suicide in later years.

115

Gene said, "I'll drive you to the bus station."

"Good. I'd like that. Thanks."

I didn't know Gene as well as I did the others. He played ball with me but was different. He wouldn't gamble or drink. Yeah, he was different.

"I wish things had worked out better for you," Gene said, as we drove off campus. "It sure has been good playing ball with you."

"Yeah," I said, looking back one more time at the college that had been my home for the last three years, "it's been fun."

"What are you going to do now?" he asked.

I wished he hadn't asked that question because that was one thing I didn't know. What was I going to do now?

He stopped at the bus station. I just sat there and leaned back for a few minutes wishing it was all a dream. I wanted to say, "Let's go back to Rogers." But I knew it was over. I would never go back. I finally turned to thank him. He had tears in his eyes.

"You OK?" I asked.

"Yeah, but remember, Wales, I'll be praying for you," he said. He then drove off, gone forever. I ached.

I never saw Gene again, but I would like to. He left a lasting impression on me. I'd like to thank him for being my friend and for praying for me.

I heard he became a preacher, and I'm sure he was the best.

23
June Bug

✜

Home was my security. The house didn't look like much. It was at the end of a dirt road, unpainted, and had a tin roof. The roof gave a wonderful sound when it rained. There's no better sleeping than a gentle rain on a tin roof. My brother and I used to lie in bed on rainy nights and just listen. At that moment, there was nothing in the whole world as peaceful as listening to the rain on the roof.

Mama was making supper when I walked in. She gave me a hug that meant more than all the girls I had hugged in all my life. She looked at me and asked, "Are you all right?"

"I am now," I replied, for Mama was my security. She wasn't surprised to see me since I came home often. I didn't tell her the reason I was home.

"Supper's almost done," she called to me as I went up to my bedroom. Flopping down across my bed, I wondered what to tell her. She'd been hurt enough, and I sure didn't want to add anymore. I wanted to die. How could I tell her I lost my basketball scholarship and was kicked out of college?

Mama was so proud of my being student body president and having a desk right in the dean of men's office. Why had I changed the record of those two girls who had too many class cuts to get their grades? I didn't know the dean had already added their cuts before he left me alone that day in his office. He had caught me red handed.

If I hadn't been caught, he was onto my case anyway. He suspected I was selling white whiskey, but his only evidence was smelling it in my room.

"Come on down, sonny boy," Mama called. "Everything is hot; it won't be near as good if it gets cold."

117

How Mama got money to put food on the table with Daddy dead and no income always amazed me. She had cooked great northern beans, potato salad, pork chops, fresh tomatoes, cucumbers, onions, and her famous cornbread, served with all the buttermilk we could drink.

My brother and I would put cornbread in our buttermilk, mix it up, and eat it out of the glass. When I finished, I thought I was going to pop. I sat there and just moaned. Nothing would make Mama happier than to know her boys were full.

"You both go sit on the front porch, let your supper go down, then I'll bring dessert."

We never asked if we could clear the table or wash dishes and Mama never asked us. We just wobbled out the front door to the porch. I sat in the swing and my brother in our daddy's old rocking chair. I was safe in my house, on that porch, in that swing, and full of Mama's cooking. All my problems were forgotten.

My younger brother Hulon, who was ten, had caught a June bug. He tied a string to its back leg and the other end to his chair. I watched the big bug fly off. It went only as far as the length of the string. As it pulled on the string, its little wings went a hundred miles an hour trying to get free, but it was useless. Soon it flew back to the chair. After several tries, it gave up and settled there next to Hulon who enjoyed the victory.

Mama came out with two big bowls of banana pudding. She gave one to my brother and handed me the other. I asked, "Where's yours?"

"Too full. I'll eat mine tomorrow."

She wouldn't. She knew we would eventually eat it for her.

"This is good, Mama. How do you make it so delicious and runny?" I asked.

"I guess experience. When you've done it all your life, it seems natural."

Mama never used a recipe to cook or bake. She cooked by taste. If it tasted good to her, she knew everybody would love it.

By the time I ate the huge bowl of pudding, I was stuffed and miserable.

It was getting late, so I asked my brother if he was going to let the bug go.

"No, sir, this bug's gonna stay with me 'til it dies."

When he went to bed, the June bug went with him.

Mama sat in the swing next to me. I put my arm around her, and we sat there not saying a word, just enjoying the summer night. It wasn't hot, and the fireflies dancing made a pretty picture. There must have been a million out in the field. The old swing needed grease. The squeak of its rusty chains sounded like sweet music to us. Mama and I just sat and swung, looked out at the night and listened to the crickets.

"Getting late," Mama said and patted my hand. "Don't you think we ought to turn in?"

"Yeah, I'm pretty tired," I yawned and streched. "Thanks for the supper, Mama. It was great as always."

I started to get up. Mama took me by the arm. "Are you sure you're all right, sonny boy?"

I sat back down. "You know, Mama, I'm like that June bug Hulon has."

"What do you mean, son?"

I replied, "I feel like something has a hold of me and won't let go."

"Whatever it is, in time, it'll let go," she said.

"No, Mama, it's not going to ever let me go. I'll be like the June bug. To be free, I'll have to die first."

24
"It's De Land"

I needed a job since I wasn't going to school. Somebody told me Mr. Evans was looking for help in clearing off land on his farm. That wasn't exactly what I wanted, but it was the only work available around Tallapoosa.

I walked three miles from my house to his to ask about the job. I found him home and inquired if he had hired anyone to clear his property.

"I need one more man. I've already lined up a black man who's good with an axe. Think you could keep up with him?" he asked. "Don't need anybody who will drag. It's hard work, and I expect a good eight hours a day. You ever cut wood before?"

"Yes, sir," I said. "I cut wood at home for my folks and cut kindling for a few widow women."

"Lotta difference in cutting kindling and cutting trees," he told me. "How much you expect to get paid?"

I replied, "Whatever the job pays."

"I promised the black man $3 a day. Wouldn't be right not to pay you the same, you being white. Is that fair?"

"Yes, sir, that's just fine," I answered.

"You meet us in front of the post office at 6:30 in the morning and I'll carry you out to the farm. You understand, 6:30," he said.

"Yes, sir, I'll be there," I said. "Mr. Evans?"

"Yes, what is it?"

"Would you let me have $1 in advance? You see, I'll need to buy me some lunch to take out there"

"Don't like to advance anybody before he ever starts work, but here's a dollar," he replied. "I'll only pay you $2 tomorrow. Fair?"

"Yes, sir, fair enough," I said.

I stopped at McKibbon's Grocery Store, bought a large can of pork and beans, a can of Vienna sausages, and a small box of soda crackers. Now I was ready to cut down trees, or so I thought.

The next morning I saw a big black man sitting on the post office steps. I knew he was a tree cutter because he had a big axe sitting between his legs. It had razor sharp double blades.

"You cuttin' for Mr. Evans?" I asked.

"Yes, sir. I sure am," he replied. "And what about you?"

"Yes, he hired me just last night," I answered.

I showed him my axe. I could tell he wasn't impressed.

He said, "Afraid you ain't gonna cut many trees with that."

"Why?" I asked.

"First of all, it's too light for tree cutting, and it looks mighty dull. But I'll take care of that when we get to Mr. Evans' farm. What's your name?"

"Goebel," I replied.

"Your daddy Vick Goebel?" he asked.

"No, sir, my daddy was the old man," I said.

"You mean the old man who ran the meat market was your daddy?" he asked.

"Yes, sir," I said.

"Why, I didn't know he had a boy as young as you," he said.

"There's two more younger than me," I told him.

"Land sakes! I never knew that," he exclaimed.

"What's your name?" I asked.

"Robinson," he said. "I stay out on Steadman Road. Been there most of my life. My daddy moved us there from Fruithurst, Alabama, as sharecroppers to a white family."

"Yeah, I know where Fruithurst is," I said.

Mr. Evans drove up right on time. He asked Robinson if we'd met.

"Yes, sir, we're already acquainted," he said.

"Reckon he'll be able to do the work?" Mr. Evans asked.

"He'll do just fine," Robinson replied.

That made me feel good, hearing him say that.

"Get up in the front seat, young man," Mr. Evans said. "Robinson, you take the back."

Although he was older, that didn't matter. Blacks always sat in the back in those days. Nobody thought much about it, except we never thought to ask the blacks how they felt. That's the way it was in those times, not only in Tallapoosa, but everywhere.

"Well, here you are," Mr. Evans said when he stopped on the side of the road. He stretched out his arm and pointed to the woods. "All those trees and that underbrush have to go before you finish."

My heart sank. I looked at the proposed field and felt like someone on the Georgia chain gang facing a life sentence. Why, I thought, it would take us forever to clear that much land.

Mr. Evans gave Robinson final instructions and said he'd be back at 5:30 to get us.

"Well, whatcha say we git to it," Robinson said. "These trees won't fall with us lookin' at 'em."

He grabbed my axe and took out his file. In a few minutes, it was sharper than when it was new.

"You take that tree," he told me, "and I'll take this one, and before you know it, we'll have this land ready for Mr. Evans to plant cotton."

Robinson was one of the most enthusiastic men I had ever seen. He went to cutting and singing all at the same time. But me, I started cutting and complaining. In a few minutes, I heard his tree fall. I was astonished. I hadn't made a good-sized dent in mine. Then another tree fell. It went that way all morning.

"Lunch time!" called Robinson.

I dragged myself over to one of the felled trees and took a seat. Robinson sat down next to me. I opened my can of pork and beans and Vienna sausages. Robinson took out a can from his pocket and ran a key around it. When it opened, I saw six little fish, heads and all.

"What's that?" I asked.

"Why, that's sardines," he said. "You never seen sardines before?"

"No, sir," I replied. "Don't believe I would care for them."

"Mighty tasty," he commented.

"You gonna cook 'em?" I asked.

"Already cooked," was his reply.

"Don't look cooked to me," I said.

"Yes, sir, these little fellows are all ready to be eaten," he said. "Sure you won't have one?"

"I'm sure," I replied.

He put the first one on his tongue, rolled it around in his mouth, and held it there awhile. When I saw his Adam's apple go up and down, I knew it was gone. I was so taken aback watching him eat, I had almost forgotten my lunch. Mama had cooked me a lot of great meals in my lifetime which I ate with great relish, but I have never seen anyone enjoy a meal more than Robinson with his little can of sardines.

We worked hard all afternoon. For every one tree I cut, Robinson cut five or six. We stopped work at 5:00 and sat on stumps waiting for Mr. Evans to carry us to town.

I didn't understand the words of the songs Mr. Robinson sang all day, but I knew they were religious. He never sang the same one twice. He was the happiest man I'd ever seen.

After several days of cutting, he suggested, as if it would benefit us both, "Why don't you let me cut the trees? You stack the logs and clean up the underbrush. I believe we'll get a whole lot done more quicker."

His idea was great. My hands had blisters like somebody had transplanted white marbles under my skin.

"You mean to say you'll cut the rest of these trees?" I asked.

"Yes, sir, that'll be just fine with me, if you don't have any objections," he answered.

If I had believed in angels, I would have known he was sent by God. We became friends and he talked to me like a son. One day he said, "Mr. Goebel, you better go and get yourself some more education."

"I can't go back," I replied. "They kicked me out."

"No matter what they've done, if you set your mind to it, you can do anything you want. But you have to believe that with all your heart. Now you listen and listen good. You ain't never going to make it as a tree cutter. I don't intend for you to take offense, but I'm telling you what's right. De Laud never seen fit to allow me much opportunity for schooling. I'll tell you right now if He had, I wouldn't be out here in these woods trying to feed a family on $3 a day. And when we finish here, I just don't know where my next job is coming from. But you're young and white and you ain't nobody's fool. You make up your mind what I'm telling you is the truth. You get an education. You hear me?"

"Yes, sir," I replied.

We worked every day except Sunday for three weeks. We both gave Mr. Evans eight hours as he requested. For certain, Mr. Robinson gave eight hours. My water breaks were longer than the ten minutes agreed upon, all because Mr. Robinson always suggested I sit and cool a bit longer.

"Don't want you having no heat stroke way out here," he'd say. "I wouldn't know what to do with you."

I'd sit in the shade, and he would cut and sing. He was one of the finest men I ever knew.

When we finished, we stood on a hill overlooking the land. It was hard to believe. The trees were all gone, the underbrush cleared and burned. I could tell Mr. Robinson was proud.

"Mr. Goebel," he said, "I'd never have been able to finish the job if Mr. Evans hadn't had the good sense to hire you."

Then he picked up my axe and looked at it with admiration. "I don't believe there's ever been a little axe that cut down so many trees. Uh huh, that shore is some good axe," he smiled.

When Mr. Evans picked us up, I looked back at the property. "Yes sir, it sure looks pretty," I said to myself, "thanks to Robinson."

Mr. Evans let us out at the post office. He gave us our $3, then said, "I'm going to give you both $1 extra."

Robinson tipped his old hat and thanked Mr. Evans a dozen times. "If you ever need any more cutting," he said, "come and get me."

"Why I sure will," Mr. Evans replied. "And, Goebel, what about you?"

"No, sir," Robinson spoke for me. "He's going to git his education."

Mr. Robinson and I shook hands. I really wanted to hug his neck and tell him I really loved him, but men didn't do that back when I was a boy.

"You go on and git your education," Mr. Robinson said. "And when you do, you come and visit me and tell me all about it."

"Mr. Robinson," I said, "I want to ask you a question."

"What kinda question?" he asked.

"What makes you so happy all the time?"

"Why, it's de Laud, son, it's de Laud," was his reply.

He swung his big old axe across his broad shoulders and walked right out of my life.

After I finished college, the first person I wanted to tell was Mr. Robinson. I found his home but was told he had been killed in an accident. I figured he went where those good Pentecostals went when they died. I always remember hearing them sing on Sunday as I sat out in the pasture. He would be singing his favorite, "De Laud is so good, He is so good to me."

I was about to learn that for myself.

25
Another Door

illy called you," Mama said, as I walked into the kitchen. "He called several times. You need to call him back."

"I will," I promised, as I lifted the lid on the black iron pot boiling on the wood-burning range. I didn't want to call Billy now or later. I didn't know why; usually I couldn't wait to see him. He was my best friend the three years in college. I especially liked his mama and daddy. They were a second family to me.

I just didn't want to talk to him. He was different and not the usual type of fellow I had fun with. He didn't drink and never got mad at anybody. Billy was a person who loved life and had a handle on it. He was always smiling and laughing. He never seemed to get "down." It made me feel good just to be around him.

So why was I hesitant to return his call?

The phone rang as we sat down to eat. Mama answered it, thinking it was one of her friends. My brother was too young to get calls, and most of my friends thought I was off at college.

Mama hollered from the hall where our telephone was, "It's Billy. He wants to speak to you."

"Tell him I'll call right back." I didn't want my beans and cornbread to get cold. Mama had taught me food was not as good cold as hot.

When Mama came back to the table, she looked me straight in the eye and said, "You call Billy as soon as you're through, you hear?"

"Yes, ma'am." I wondered why it was important to Mama for me to call Billy. "He just wants me to help move furniture for his daddy."

"He wants you to go to church with him," Mama replied.

I had just put a spoon of beans in my mouth. My belly laugh spewed them everywhere!

"Sorry, Mama," I said, and picked up the beans off the table cloth. "Why in the world does he want me to go to church? I didn't know he went to church!"

Billy must have been sitting by the phone because he picked it up on the first ring.

"Wales, where have you been? I've been calling since you got home!" I could tell he was excited.

"Goat, what's with this church business you've been telling Mama?" I asked, calling him by his nickname. I don't know who started it, but even today when I call him Billy, folks don't know who I'm talking about.

He said, "I'm going to be leaving in a few minutes for La Grange. I want to whip by Tallapoosa and pick you up."

"What're you gonna do in LaGrange?" I asked. I had never asked Goat this question before. Wherever he went, I always wanted to go. But Mama's words, "He wants you to go to church," rang a warning in my mind.

"They're having a revival at Trinity Methodist Church. A young fellow from Asbury College is speaking. He's great. You'll love it," he said.

"When did you start loving going to church? And what in the world makes you think I'd love going? What's got ahold of you?"

"Look, do me a favor. I'm by myself. I'm going to La Grange and need a buddy to go with me," he said.

The future Georgia state representative was beginning to show his political skill.

"What if I ride down just to keep you company, man? I'll sit in the truck until you and those Methodists get through," I said.

"Wales, there's some pretty girls attending this revival," he threw in to entice me.

We drove through Bremen, Bowden Junction, and Carrollton. The next town was La Grange. Beginning to feel nervous, I said, "Goat, let's stop at the next roadside joint. I need a Millers bad."

"Wales, you can't have a beer now; you'd smell up the church," he said.

127

"Who said I was going to church?" I asked. "You are the one going to church. I am the one who's gonna sit in this here truck while you find yourself a girl or get religion or whatever goes on in there."

We stopped at a pretty little white frame church building sitting on a corner in La Grange. There were lots of people going in.

"Go on, Goat. I'll be sittin' right here when you're finished," I said.

"Wales, what are you afraid of?"

"Nothing, but if I were, it wouldn't be folks in church," I replied.

Two of the prettiest girls in town walked toward the church. They were dressed in freshly starched and ironed dresses, probably made of material from the cotton mills there in La Grange. I watched them go in. "You know those girls, Goat?" I asked.

"One is studying art in Atlanta. I don't know the other," he replied.

I noticed they were walking. "After church, maybe they'd like two nice boys to drive them home," I said.

"You coming in or not?" Goat asked.

"I'll be right here," I said and slouched down in the seat to wait.

Billy slammed his door and was the last one to walk in the church.

"Blessed Assurance, Jesus is Mine," rang out from the church. The beautiful notes resounded into the street and surrounded me and the pickup. The singing reminded me of the Pentecostal church across the pasture from our house. In the summertime, they used to open the windows of the church. As I mentioned before, nobody could sing as loud as the Pentecostals, not even the Baptists. As a boy, I would sit out in the pasture and listen. I never went to their church, but I was faithful on Sunday to be out there listening. I could hear the preacher say he was going to call down the Spirit. I never knew what happened in there, but they were the happiest people in Tallapoosa.

Suddenly, there was a knock on the truck door. Startled, I turned and there stood the good-looking art student from Atlanta.

"Goat said you would like to take us home after church. Is that right?" she asked.

"Yes, it sure is." My heart began to pound. I was flabbergasted to see that pretty little thing just standing there.

"He said you weren't feeling too well but would be right on in. Are you better now?" she asked in honeyed tones.

"Yes," I said, sitting tall. "I feel fine."

"Well, come on. Church is starting."

I opened the door, and she reached and took my hand. I thought I'd melt.

"I haven't seen you at the revival before," she said.

"This is my first time," I replied.

She asked, "You like going to church?"

"Oh, sure, I even sit outside sometime just listening to what's going on inside," I told her.

We walked through the front door into the sanctuary. I was about to be shown another Door, and for once in my life it wouldn't be the back door.

26
Something Was Different

✣

A feeling of awe came over me when the art student and I walked into the sanctuary. Perhaps it was because of my deep respect that this was, in a sense, the house of God.

Goat had been watching the door. When he saw us walk in, he motioned to us to come sit by him and the other girl. He was gloating because he knew I couldn't refuse a pretty face.

A curly-headed man sang a solo. As he sang, I forgot about his looks because the words stunned me. "Just a closer walk with Thee. I am weak, but Thou art strong. Jesus keep me from all wrong; I'll be satisfied as long as I walk close to Thee."

Before the song was finished, I began to feel at ease. A quiet rest settled over my soul. My heart was warmed by the song.

I listened intently during what they called "testimony time." Some of the young people my age stood up and talked about Jesus like He was their friend. I would never have admitted it to anyone, but I said to myself, "I would give anything if I could do that." Then I remembered James' words back in high school while we were sitting in the far corner of our football field with a couple of pints of port, "Wales, you might as well forget about God. He doesn't let people like us in heaven." What he said hurt me deeply, but I knew it was true. As I listened to the church sing those old, wonderful hymns, I thought maybe there was a way for even me to get into heaven. At first, I felt out of place, but now I was becoming comfortable.

At some point in the service, the young preacher from Asbury brought a brief message. It seemed like he was talking right to me.

At the end of his sermon, the preacher said, "We will sing two stanzas of 'Just As I Am.' If you are here tonight and will take Jesus as your Savior, please come to the altar and I, along with others, will pray you through."

The first stanza was sung. Nobody moved. My heart was beating so hard I thought it would come out of my chest. My hands were dripping sweat like bullets.

When we were halfway through the second stanza, the young preacher pleaded, "If anyone needs to trust Jesus, come now while there is still time."

I turned to Billy and asked if he would like to go down and get prayed through. He shook his head "no." He didn't know he should have walked to the altar with me. I wasn't all that familiar with the song they were singing but knew my time was running out. A tall skinny boy about my age was standing behind me. I turned to him and said, "You look like you need to go down and talk to the preacher. If you're afraid to go, I'll go with you." He looked at me like I was crazy.

The song was now over, and books were being put in the racks. I wished I had never walked in that church. I was miserable before I came, and now I felt worse.

A spark of hope flamed in my heart when the preacher said, "Before I close with the benediction, would you take your song books and let's sing one more verse. In my spirit, I feel there's someone God is dealing with. I want to apologize for delaying you, but it'll take only a couple of minutes more."

Everyone reached for their song books, and the piano player made the music sound as if it were right out of Heaven. "Just as I am Thou wilt receive, wilt welcome, pardon, cleanse, relieve, because Thy promise I believe." It would be years before I learned how much the writer of that song and I had in common.

"I don't know who is resisting God's wonderful love, but I can tell you are one unhappy person. If you will only trust Jesus, He will change all that," the preacher said, trying to encourage me, only he didn't know it was me he was talking to.

"O Lamb of God, I come, I come!" the song's invitation called out to me. I stood up, not paying any attention to anyone else, not even Billy or the tall boy, and moved into the aisle. Walking to the altar, I felt my heart would break with joy even as tears coursed down my face. I took the young preacher by the hand and he told me, "Ask Jesus to come into your heart and forgive your sins."

I did! All of a sudden, all of my 22 years of sin seemed to be lifted off my shoulders. I knelt at the altar and people surrounded me, mostly young people. When I looked up, there stood Billy and the tall boy smiling and crying. I wasn't ashamed of my tears when I saw most of the people crying, too. I asked Billy, "Did you get saved?"

"I did about two weeks ago back at Rockmart!" That was his home church. He put his arms around me in a bear hug and said, "I love you, Wales."

I hugged him back, and before the church closed its doors I hugged everybody there. There has never been so much crying and hugging as there was that special Saturday night. It would be years before I learned John Wesley felt the same way I did the night he was converted. I know exactly what he meant when he wrote "my heart was strangely warmed when I trusted in Christ alone to pay the penalty for my sin."

I thank God every day for the little cotton mill Methodist church in La Grange, Georgia, that loved souls and for a little preacher boy who was so close to God he could say, "In my spirit...God is dealing with someone here tonight. Won't you come to Jesus?"

And come I did.

27
I Sat Down Next To Jesus

✛

W here're we going?" Billy asked, as we loaded up the girls to carry them home. The small pickup cab wasn't big enough for us to sit side by side, so the pretty art student sat on my lap. At that moment, I realized I was changed. Her being there didn't faze me.

"Home," I said, without a moment's hesitation.

"What about these girls?" he asked and looked at me with the biggest question I'd ever seen registered on his face. They were my reason for going in church, so how could we just go home now?

"I would like to go home, if that's OK with y'all," I said.

"Sure," the art student responded. "If that's what you would rather do, then you should go home."

She managed to squeeze between the other girl and me after the doors closed. We almost pushed Billy out of the driver's seat, so for his comfort and our safety, we dropped both girls off at one of their homes.

Driving back to Tallapoosa, Billy remembered I had wanted to stop for a beer. He asked if I was still thirsty.

"No, thanks," I said.

We didn't talk much going home. We were subdued like there had been a death. Come to think of it, there was. Not one I recognized at the time, but it was what Paul wrote about, dying to yourself and Jesus living in your heart.

It was after midnight when we pulled into my driveway. Billy asked if I wanted to talk awhile.

"Naw, not now, Goat, I want to tell Mama."

I got out, but Billy sat there as I walked to our steps. Turning, I said, "Billy, thanks for tonight. I will always be indebted to you."

He said, "I love you, Wales," before driving off.

"Yeah, I know it." I answered.

Mama had been in bed since sundown. She had to because her work started before the sun came up.

But she never went to sleep until all her children were home and safe in their beds.

I knelt by her bed. "Mama, you awake?" I asked.

"Yes, are you all right?" she answered.

"Mama, I've been saved."

"You've been what?"

"I've been saved."

"Blow your breath," she demanded, rising up on one elbow.

When she didn't smell beer, she asked me to blow harder. I nearly blew her out of bed.

"What do you mean you've been saved?" she asked. I could see her brow knit together, and her eyes looked deep into mine.

When Mama was a young girl, she had been baptized in the First Christian Church. She didn't attend services as much as she would like to, and she didn't know the difference between baptism and salvation.

I said, "Mama, I have Jesus in my heart, and when I die, I'm going to heaven."

"What in the world are you talking about?" she asked.

"Well, I went with Billy to church like you asked me to. And, Mama, when I sat down in the pew, I sat down next to Jesus."

Mama hugged me, and then she cried.

"Mama."

"Yes?" she said.

"I want you to go with me to heaven, because heaven wouldn't mean much to me if you weren't there."

"You go to bed, Wales. We'll talk about it tomorrow."

I lay in bed too excited to sleep. I kept turning toward the little window and saying, "Come on sun. Show yourself. I've got a lot of folks I need to talk to." It seemed it took 24 hours for the sun to rise that night.

We had a cow we affectionately named Pet. I had another name for her that I can't mention. On cold winter mornings, I would rather be under my warm quilts than milking "Pet." But my job was milking and milk her I did.

This morning, I was up and downstairs before Mama called. I picked up the milk bucket and looked on the stove. She was cooking my favorite breakfast—a big hoecake. It's sort of like a biscuit, only it's cooked in a pan by itself. It's mashed almost flat and browned on both sides. I liked to open it up and watch steam rise as I poured homemade melted butter over it. My mouth watered thinking about how I would bathe that hoecake with our Georgia sugar-cane syrup.

I ran out and milked Pet so fast it's a wonder she didn't dry up. It wasn't just the breakfast that made me hurry. I couldn't wait to talk to Mama about Jesus.

I sat the milk bucket on the counter next to the sink and sat down to eat my hoecake. Mama had a cup of coffee.

"Mama, this is the best day of my life," I said.

"That's wonderful," she replied. "I'm so happy for you."

"Mama, I want you to ask Jesus to come into your heart."

"You go on to work, or you will be late," she answered.

"What about Jesus, Mama?" I asked.

"We'll talk about it tonight," she said.

"You could die today," I told her. "It will only take a minute. I just asked Him to come in my heart last night, and He did. It surely would please me if you would."

"Here's your lunch," she said. "You'd better get going."

A terrible thought ran through my mind, "If Mama, who loves me more than anybody in the whole world, wouldn't pray with me to receive Christ, the folks at Sam's beer joint and Cartwright's poolroom might not either!"

That thought broke my heart.

28
Tears In The Beer

The Methodist minister in the First Church in Tallapoosa asked me to teach the young people's Sunday school class. It must have been frustrating to the class, because I had never taught before and really didn't know much. Every Sunday, I gave my testimony and told them they all needed to be out witnessing, winning the town for Christ. They all agreed Tallapoosa, with all the pool halls and beer joints, really needed saving. Looking back, I don't know if any of the young people in my class really had Christ in their lives.

I went to the pastor's office nearly every day to ask questions about the Bible. When I found he took Mondays off, I thought, how can a minister take a day off when so many people need to know Christ?

First and foremost, my burden was Mama. I spent hours around an old tree stump in our back yard praying for Mama's conversion. Daddy had cut down the tree, and I picked the stump as my prayer altar. I didn't close my eyes but looked out into the woods and talked to God.

Mama, however, wasn't the first person the Lord let me see respond to my witnessing.

The day after my conversion, I went to see Miss Flo. I had known her and her family for years. She was one person in town who had been especially nice to me. She lived with a fellow named Dad. I guess they were husband and wife. I just never knew for sure. Dad owned one of the beer joints on Highway 78, and Miss Flo was the bartender. He loved fishing and spent most of his time on the river. Whenever I went in for a draft beer, Miss Flo was always behind the counter.

I walked into their bar early that first morning because I wanted to lead Miss Flo to Jesus. They had a bargain on until noon—a whole frosty mug full of draft beer for a nickel. Three older men were already there taking advantage of the bargain beer. Miss Flo automatically reached in the cooler for a mug.

"I don't want any beer, Miss Flo, thanks," I said. "I want to tell you what happened to me last night."

She sat down on her stool and said, "What is it, Wales?"

One thing I'd learned when I sold beer at Whitie's was that you have to listen to some sad stories. I guess that's where the saying "crying in your beer" came from.

Miss Flo listened at first when I started telling her my story. I hadn't gotten too far when two of the men got up and left. They hadn't even finished their beers.

That's strange, I thought.

As I talked, I could tell Miss Flo was not paying attention. But I noticed the one man who had not left had tears in his eyes. I turned and apologized for upsetting him.

He said, "I was reminded by what you were telling Miss Flo of how many times my Mama shared those same words with me."

I said, "Then you're not a Christian?"

He broke down and cried harder. Between wiping his tears and blowing his nose, he told me he was not. I simply told him how I bowed my head and asked the Lord to forgive my sins and to come into my heart, and He came in like He promised.

"He'll do the same for you if you want Him to," I told the man.

He said that was his heart's desire. Right there, that bar was transformed into a sanctuary. The man prayed a simple childlike prayer, "Lord, thank you for sending this man to remind me of my mother's words. I give you my heart. Please forgive my sins."

He walked out with a smile on his face and a light in his eyes. He didn't finish his beer either. I never saw him again. Just Miss Flo and I were left. I looked at her and said, "Wasn't that wonderful?"

"What's happened to you, Wales?"

"I've got what you'd call religion," I said.

"I think it's wonderful, and I hope you keep it forever," she said and slapped her hand on the bar.

"I will," I replied confidently.

"Best you do your preaching outside than in here." She picked up the half empty mugs left by the men and put them in the sink. "It's not good for business."

"What about you?" I asked.

"Not now" is all she said.

I went back often over the next 30 years. Miss Flo never prayed with me. She was always kind and listened. She had the excuse so many use—too many hypocrites in the church.

A friend called me when she died.

I surely did love Miss Flo. She let me preach my first sermon standing at her bar.

29
Spirit in the Trunk

✜

The old tree stump had always been a special play place. Now it was my sanctuary. It was surrounded by other large trees towering over me. When the sun filtered through the green leaves and its brilliant rays fell on my prayer stump, it was as glorious as any cathedral. I sat down and praised God for saving me and asked Him not to forget about saving Mama.

I sat there in my private place of worship and asked God for a special request. I wanted Him to get me a Bible.

It was only a few weeks after I had been saved when this desire to read the Bible filled my mind. Surely the best place to find one would be at one of our local churches. So I headed for the largest church in town, the First Baptist. I had only been in it once, and that's when I wanted to date a girl in high school. The only way her mother approved of her going out with me was if I took her to Sunday night church. That didn't cause me a problem; I would still get to walk her home. I don't remember much of the service, because my mind was on the long walk to her house.

The Baptist preacher was tall like me. He met me at the door of his office and kindly invited me in. When I sat down, he wanted to know how he could be of help. I told him I had been saved a few weeks before and needed a Bible.

He asked, "Have you been baptized or joined a church?"

"No, sir, not yet," I said. "But I plan to. Could you help me to get a Bible?"

He said I should consider joining the church first. I was frustrated and soon got up, thanked him, and left.

The First Methodist was the second-largest church in Tallapoosa.

Since I was converted in a church of that denomination, surely I could get a Bible there. But, no, there were no extra Bibles on hand.

The only thing I knew about the First Presbyterian Church was it was small and sat on a corner two blocks from my high school. I had noticed that they had only a few cars parked out front on Sundays. I didn't know of a young person who attended it. But I was desperate for a Bible. It took several visits before I found the pastor in his office. When I explained what I wanted, he asked why I was so anxious to own a Bible. I told him of my conversion to Christ a few weeks earlier, and now I wanted to know God better.

"What do you mean by conversion?" he asked.

I went through my story of how I was saved in a little Methodist church in La Grange, Georgia. He asked if it wasn't a Baptist rather than a Methodist.

"No, sir," I replied. "It was Trinity Methodist Church."

"Strange," he responded. "I thought only the Baptists had those kinds of experiences."

"Whatcha mean by 'experience'?" I asked.

"Those emotional experiences they have," he replied.

"No, sir, you misunderstood. I didn't have an emotional experience. I got saved," I said.

"It's all the same," he answered.

"How 'bout a Bible?" I asked.

"Don't know of one right off. I'll look around. If I find one, I'll let you know."

As I started to the door, he called out, "What did you say your name was?"

"Wales, Wales Goebel," I answered.

He counseled me, "Wales, don't get too carried away with your experience or the saved business. You'll find out it's not all you think it is."

"That's why I want a Bible," I said. "I want to know what I've got."

Word got around town that I had been saved. One friend, Garland Cain, who I had led to Christ, told everybody about his conversion and mine. There was an older couple who were known as dedicated Christians that heard the news about me. Mrs. Jackson came looking for me because Mr. Jackson wanted to hear my testimony. She found me at the baseball field watching a practice. She called a boy standing near where she parked her big Chrysler and asked him to go get me.

"Hello, Mrs. Jackson. What can I do for you?" I asked, leaning down to the car window.

"Wales, Arlen wants to talk to you. Will you go to the house with me now?"

"Sure. I'd love to." I knew just about everyone in Tallapoosa and knew the Jacksons were real Christians. They lived in one of those big old Georgian homes that I passed on my way anywhere in town.

Mrs. Jackson took me into the living room, and I'll never forget the Persian rug that covered the floor. Mr. Jackson's eyes were bad, but he stood up and pumped my hand. "Have a seat, son. I want to hear your testimony."

I sat on the old antique couch and told them about sitting down next to Jesus. When I finished, Mr. Jackson said, "Mama, let's pray for Wales. Come over here, son, and kneel by my chair, so I can put my hands on your head."

It was the sweetest prayer I ever heard. At last, I had found some people in Tallapoosa to have Christian fellowship with. After prayer, I told them of my desire to have a Bible.

Mr. Jackson said, "Wales, whatever is in your power to do, God expects you to do it. What's not in your power, then He will do it."

As I walked toward my house, I thought about what he said. He was a great Christian so I remembered his words. I would do exactly what he said. After that, I stopped by their house often to pray with them. Once Mr. Jackson said, "Wales, Mama and I believe God has called you to preach."

"I don't know about being a preacher, Mr. Jackson. I'll have to think about it." I was surprised.

"My wife and I know it. We're so sure about it we'll pay your way to seminary."

Next time I saw Garland, I told him what the Jacksons had said. "But I'm not sure He has called me to be a preacher."

"I believe God has called me to preach, Wales. Do you think Mr. Jackson would send me to seminary?"

"I don't know, Garland. Let's go ask him."

Mr. Jackson said, "I made Wales the offer because God laid it on my heart. I'll ask Him if He wants me to do the same for you."

The Jacksons didn't feel led to finance Garland's seminary training, but he went on to become a Baptist preacher anyway.

I decided not to ask any more preachers for a Bible. I would just go directly to God, which is how I ended up on my prayer stump asking God to bring me a Bible.

Soon after my prayer, I was standing on the corner at Smith's Cafe. A car pulled into Fats' Service Station across the street. While Fats filled the car with gas, the driver told him he was from Atlanta and was in this area selling Bibles. Fats nearly spilled the gas on the ground. He wasn't the kind of man who read the Bible, but he knew of my search for one.

I saw Fats with his mouth gaping open, pointing at me with one hand and holding the dripping gas hose with the other. Then the salesman rapidly walked toward me. I thought he must have been mad at me the way he rushed over.

"Hear you looking to buy a Bible." He stuck out his right hand and vigorously pumped mine.

My heart nearly came out of my chest, "Yes sir, you know where I might find one?" I asked, now gripping his hand firmly like he might get away.

"Sure do," he beamed. "In the trunk of my car."

Bootleggers kept their spirits in their trunks; now here was a Bible salesman with another kind of Spirit in his car trunk.

"What kind you looking for?" he thumped me on the back as we recrossed the street to the filling station.

"The bigger, the better, " I answered. "Something people can see when I walk in the poolroom."

"Got just the one."

He opened his trunk. Never in my life had anything looked so beautiful. A whole trunk full of Bibles!

"How 'bout this one?" he asked.

He handed me a Bible so big that when I took it, it nearly weighted me down.

"What kind of Bible is this?" I asked.

"It's a family Bible. You can keep all your records in it," he said. "You won't find a nicer Bible anywhere. And I'll let you have it at a good price."

"It's nice, but I need something I can carry around." I handed it back to him.

"Oh," he said, "you want a church Bible."

"Maybe, let's see one," I said.

He took out the prettiest Bible I had ever seen. It was in an attractive pasteboard box with angels painted on it. I thought all Bibles were black. But not this one. It was brown and the outside edge of the pages was all gold-covered. It had little thumb tabs at each book so I could quickly find the right page if the preacher asked us to open to such-and-such a passage.

When he told me to hold it in my hands I was a little afraid. But when I did, there was such a feeling of excitement, I could hardly contain myself. On the cover was a picture.

"Whose picture?" I asked.

"Jesus," the salesman said reverently.

"Jesus? I didn't know there were any pictures of Jesus."

"That one you are holding in your hand is the last one. When it is gone, there'll be no more," he said with conviction.

I was breathless.

"You wouldn't part with this, would you?" I felt a fool for asking.

He looked at me; then he looked away. Finally, he said, "You really want to buy this Bible, don't you?"

"If there is any way I could own this Bible, I would be eternally grateful."

"How much money do you have?" he asked.

I looked in my pocket and came up with exactly $2.

"Is that enough?" I asked.

"Not exactly. You need $20 more."

"But I just don't have it," I said.

"Can you borrow it from your daddy?" he asked.

"He's dead," I replied.

"How 'bout your Mama?"

"Don't guess Mama ever had $20 in her life," I replied.

"Could I trust you?" he asked.

"You couldn't before, but since I've been saved, you can," I answered.

"If I leave the Bible with you, would you send me $2 a week?" he asked.

"Yes sir, even if I don't eat, you'll get your money."

He handed me the Bible. My own Bible! We shook hands on the transaction. As he started to close the trunk of his car, I asked, "Reckon I could have the box with the angels on top?"

He handed it to me and asked, "You know who those two angels are?"

"No, sir, I sure don't."

"Gabriel and Michael," he said.

"Any other pictures of them?" I asked.

"No, you got the last one."

I thought how blessed I really was.

30
Cost Me My Chesterfields

✛

"hy do you smoke if you are such a fine Christian?" Mama
asked, with a note of skepticism in her voice.

You could have knocked me over with a feather when she
said that. God had taken away all my desire for alcohol, and
cursing left my mouth as if a knife had cut it out. I was staying out of
trouble, spending more time with her than I ever had in my life. I
didn't know it, but Mama was coming under conviction. She was grasp-
ing at straws to feel secure in her good works. She smoked.

"What's wrong with smoking?" I asked, when I recovered myself.

I had been smoking as long as I could remember. I started as a boy by
picking rabbit tobacco and rolling it in paper from the Sears and
Roebuck catalog. Our catalog was used around the house for many
things. We were big recyclers before the word was invented. We hardly
ever ordered anything from it because Mama didn't have money to buy
store-bought stuff. She made our clothes, curtains for the house, quilts
for the beds, and even slip covers for our furniture with her pedal
sewing machine.

Robert, my older half-brother, lived with us. There was no room for
him inside our house, so he slept on the back porch. He slept there in
the cold of winter and the heat of summer. Best I remember, I never
heard him complain. He was what people called a "good soul."

He owned a little cigarette-making machine. He put enough tobacco
in it for one cigarette, put a piece of cigarette paper on the roller, and
gave the handle a pull. Out rolled the prettiest cigarette you ever saw.
He wet one end of the paper with his tongue to make it stick and twisted the other end with his fingers. Next, he got a match out of the big
matchbox by the range and scratched the head on the leg of his overalls. He'd touch the flame to the twisted end of the freshly made

cigarette, draw in deeply until the end glowed red and hot. To us, that was smoking at its very best.

When we had a little money, we went to Mr. G.B. Evans' grocery store and for ten cents bought a pack of 20 cigarettes. We called these "tailor made." My preference was a brand called Chesterfield.

By the time I was converted, I was totally addicted to tobacco.

"So what's the big deal, Mama, about smoking?" I asked.

"Real Christians ought not to smoke," she said.

Well, I thought, one thing I know, and that is I'm a real Christian.

The next day, I went to see the Methodist preacher. He was in his office, and I asked for a minute of his time.

Steps on the outside of the church led right into his small office, which really had no privacy. He always seemed glad to meet with me, probably because he had never seen anyone quite like me. I was ignorant of the Bible but so anxious to know things. In a way, I'd become his project.

"What can I do for you, Wales?" he asked, standing up and shaking my hand.

He sat at his desk, and I perched on the edge of a metal folding chair. I leaned forward and earnestly asked, "Preacher, can you tell me where in the Bible it says it's wrong to smoke Chesterfields?"

He leaned back in his chair suppressing a chuckle, afraid he'd embarrass me if he laughed. He had to make do with a big grin.

"I don't know of any specific verse that speaks about Chesterfields," he answered. His eyes were filled with merriment. "Why do you ask?"

"Well, sir, you know how I've been trying to get Mama saved. About the time I think she's ready, she comes out with some crazy question I can't answer," I said.

"Like what?"

"Well, yesterday. She said if I was a real Christian, I wouldn't smoke these Chesterfields," I said and pulled a pack out of my shirt pocket.

He looked at me for a moment; his laughter was gone. He realized I was serious. Sincere concern covered his face as he replied, "Wales, which is more important, your cigarettes or your Mama's soul?"

He didn't have to say anything more. I thanked him, got up, walked out of his office, and ran all the way home.

I was nearly out of breath as I walked into the kitchen. Mama was standing at the sink washing dishes.

"Who're you running from?" she asked.

"Nobody. I just couldn't wait to tell you I'm a real Christian."

"What are you saying?" she asked.

"See these Chesterfields?" I said. "I'm going to put them in the fireplace and never smoke again. 'Cause, like you said, a real Christian doesn't smoke."

"Don't put them in no fireplace," she said. "Put them on the mantel. You'll get to craving one soon, and you'll be back."

"No, Mama, I'll never smoke again." But out of respect for Mama, I put them on the mantel.

It has been over forty years since that day. I never went back to cigarettes, not because of the Bible, but because Mama said real Christians don't smoke. One thing I knew, I was a real Christian, and if it cost me my Chesterfields, I gladly gave them up.

31
Praying in the Boiler Room

✤

'll never forget how hard it was to quit smoking, but despite withdrawals, all I needed to do was think about what the preacher said, "Which is more important, your cigarettes, or your Mama's soul?"

Mama asked me a couple of times if I was smoking behind her back.

"No, ma'am, you said real Christians don't smoke."

"Uh-huh," was all she said.

I would go out to my tree-stump altar and spend the longest time praying. My praying wasn't what folks called real praying because I didn't get on my knees or close my eyes. I just had a conversation with the Lord. The longer I talked, the more confidence I had God was going to save Mama.

The thought came to me to go see Mrs. Hittie Smith and have her pray for Mama. She and her husband ran one of the two dry-cleaning plants in town. Theirs was on the main street. I passed it two or three times a day when I was in school. Mr. Otis Smith usually stood on the sidewalk outside the plant and spoke to all of us kids who walked by on the way to school.

Mrs. Hittie was behind the cash register waiting on a customer when I went to pray with her. "When you're finished, can I talk to you?" I asked.

She replied, "It'll just be a minute."

Mr. Otis came in and asked if he could help me.

"No, sir, I want to speak to Mrs. Hittie," I said.

"Heard you gave them fire and brimstone at the church Sunday," he said.

"You didn't come?" I asked.

"No," he said. "Wish I had, from all the good reports I've been getting. They say you're going to be the next Billy Graham."

"That sure would be nice," I said.

I asked Mr. Otis how long he had been a Christian.

"All my life, I reckon," was his reply. I didn't know then that that wasn't a good answer. Later, I learned nobody's a Christian from birth.

Mrs. Hittie put her big arm around me and told me how proud she was of me. Now Mrs. Hittie was a real Christian.

"What can I do for you, Wales?" she asked.

"Well, two things," I said. "One, I want you to pray for Mama."

"What's wrong? Is she ill?" she asked.

"Oh no, ma'am," I said. "You see, she thinks she's a real Christian, and she's not. I want her to go to heaven when she dies."

"Why, boy, you don't have a thing in the world to worry about," she said. "We'll just go back to the boiler room, and we'll just claim her."

The boiler room was noisy and hot, but that's the place where we claimed Mama for Jesus.

After I prayed, Mrs. Hittie cut loose like I used to hear the Pentecostals pray when I sat out in the pasture. I was strengthened when she finished. There was no way God was not going to hear that prayer. She prayed so hard, and being in the boiler room as well, she was wringing wet with sweat.

"Thank you, Mrs. Hittie," I said.

"You said there were two things," she replied.

"Yes, ma'am," I said. "Would it be all right if I told those two men who press clothes for you what Jesus has done for me?"

"Why, I don't know of any two men in Tallapoosa who need to hear about Jesus any more than they do," she said. Her face was all joy as she led me back to where they were pressing clothes.

They were both black and, as far as I knew, were fine people. But I felt the Lord wanted me to tell them about Jesus.

I spoke to the older one first. Then the younger began to listen. After a while, they just let the steam out of the presses and stood and listened. I could tell by his stare Mr. Otis wanted me to let them get on with their work.

149

I told the men how I just bowed my head and asked Jesus to forgive my sins and to come into my heart. "You could pray right now if you want to," I said. "You don't have to go to hell, just depends on what you want to do."

"Guess I want to go to heaven," the younger man told me.

"Me too," replied the older.

We all prayed together.

As I started to leave, I noticed the older man had a pack of cigarettes in his pocket.

"Now that you're a real Christian, you'll never want to smoke again," I told him.

"That would be nice," he said. "Yes, sir, that'd be real nice."

Mrs. Hittie hugged me again.

Mr. Otis seemed glad I was leaving.

32
The Holy Ghost Came Down

✛

Tuesday night after supper, I told Mama, "Mrs. Hittie asked me to come preach in her church next Sunday night. Her preacher said I could have the whole service."

Mrs. Hittie went to the First Pentecostal Church. It was the one next to our pasture where I used to sit on Sundays to listen to the singing and wait for the Holy Ghost to come down.

They built a new brick church across from Miller's Funeral Home about the time I went off to college. Mr. Todd was their preacher. His son was one of my high-school teachers and was a really handsome man. During our chapel time at school, he would play the piano and sing, "I Am a Private in The Army of The Lord." That song made a great impression on me. I didn't tell anyone, but I did want to be a soldier in the Lord's army.

At school, when we sang "Onward Christian Soldiers," I could picture myself dressed up in knight's armor, a cross on my chest, marching with the cross of Jesus. That was a seed God planted in my heart that now burst out in all of its fullness.

Mama went with me Sunday night. She knew everybody there. Guess I did, too. Most of them were old like Mama. I didn't know all their names but recognized their faces. They told Mama how proud she must be of me, and she was. Mama thought I was the finest thing that ever walked. Everybody bragging on me just endeared me to her more than ever.

Rev. Todd asked, "Wales, would you like to go into my office with a few deacons and ask the Lord for His blessings on our service."

"Sure would!" I thought to myself. Now I'll see what they mean by asking the Holy Ghost to come down. After all those years of sitting in

151

the pasture, I would see what happened.

Well, the Holy Ghost came down, but it was not as dramatic as I imagined. I had never heard men pray as sweet and as fervently as those did. They prayed for special anointing on me. When I heard godly men pray for me, it made me cry. Mr. Jackson put his arm on my shoulder and whispered softly, "Everything's all right."

Mr. Todd said they were thrilled that one of the first opportunities for me to preach would be in their church.

When church started, they must have sung for an hour. Young Mr. Todd played the piano. His wife had a round thing in her right hand with bells on it. She hit it against her other hand. The two of them made beautiful music. There was a lot of clapping. They didn't do this at the First Methodist Church. These people were what some would call "freed up." The Methodists were "stiffed up."

All the prayers and the singing reached deep into my soul. It was good to be surrounded with what my Mama called real Christians.

I can't remember what I preached or for how long. Pentecostals in Tallapoosa were not conscious of the clock like the Methodists and Baptists.

I had asked Rev. Todd, "How long am I to preach?"

"Until the Lord dries you up," he replied and slapped me on the back.

It could have been ten minutes or an hour, but knowing me, it was closer to an hour.

I had heard Billy Graham on the radio when he was in a crusade in Chattanooga, Tennessee. He gave an invitation for folks to come forward and get right with the Lord. I figured I ought to do the same. Seems like everybody in the church came to the altar. There was much crying and praying. I didn't know what to do, so I just sat in the chair behind the pulpit and watched Mama.

After the service, Mrs. Hittie grabbed me, gave me a big hug, and said, "God's got His hand on you. Don't you ever do anything to lose that touch."

"Yes, ma'am," I said.

As we walked home, Mama told me how proud she was of me.

"Mama, why didn't you come to the altar?" I asked.

"Why, I couldn't do that," she replied. "That's not my church. You know I belong to the First Christian Church."

No, I didn't understand. It would be a long time before I understood "that the natural (unsaved) person receiveth not the things of the Spirit of God" (I Corinthians 2:14a).

33
The Wedding

✤

Mama could see that I was still in love with Jean and how it hurt when my phone calls were refused. I drove over to West Georgia to see Jean only to be told by Miss Howard she did not want to see me.

When school was out, Mama called Jean in Summerville and invited her to spend a weekend with us. Jean was hesitant, but Mama insisted and asked to speak with Jean's mother.

"I'll let Jean come if you promise to be at the bus when she gets off," Mrs. Duff said.

Jean came back on the phone and said, "Mrs. Goebel, I'll come, but I want you with us all the time I'm there."

All the young converts from the Methodist revival, where I was saved, were giving their testimonies in churches and high schools all over west Georgia. They set up a big meeting at Tallapoosa High and asked me to be the "featured speaker." I was the prize convert since my life had been drastically changed.

Jean came that weekend, and I can't say which was more important, her coming or a chance to tell people about the Lord. The auditorium was packed, but the only two people I saw were Jean and Mama sitting in the crowd.

True to her word, Mama was with us every minute of Jean's stay. Jean was such a good person she didn't understand she was not a Christian. Our relationship blossomed because she could see I had changed. I wasn't the same person who had been expelled from college.

I bought a car and went to see her every weekend. I'd start out early on the 65 mile trip to Summerville and get there by 9:30. That gave us 30 minutes before Jean went to work in a dress shop. All day her mother and I talked. "You see, Mrs. Duff, the Bible says those that are in Christ are new creations. I'm a real Christian now."

"I can see that, Wales. I'm glad you and Jean are dating again."

It was hard to wait for Jean to get home. Our love was in full flower, and we planned our wedding for August 27—just three months from Jean's first visit to Tallapoosa.

"Jean, I don't have any money for a honeymoon, but my uncle said we could use his house in the Catskill Mountains if we could get there."

"Wales, I've been saving the money I made since junior high showing prize cattle. Daddy has it in savings bonds for me. I have enough for our trip and a little nest egg to help start us out. How long can we stay at your uncle's house?"

"He said we could have it for two weeks!"

Jean and I went to her mother to tell her the news. "Mrs. Duff, we want to get married the last of August. Will you give us your approval?"

"But, Jean, what about college? You've only finished one year."

"Mother, I don't want to waste Daddy's money going back to school. All I want is to be a good wife and mother."

"August doesn't give us much time to plan a wedding, Jean. Why don't you wait a while?"

"We'll only invite the family and a few close friends. I've already picked out my dress. In fact, it's on lay-a-way right now."

My family drove to Summerville for the 4:00 Sunday afternoon wedding. We planned to arrive at the Duffs around 2:00 and change into our wedding clothes. Cars were not air-conditioned back then, and August is hot in Georgia. We were making good time on the two-lane roads until slowed to a snail's pace behind a funeral procession. There must have been fifty cars behind the black hearse. The procession poked along for miles and miles and miles. The police escort wouldn't let anyone pass. Cars coming in the opposite direction stopped, and people on the side of the road took off their hats and waited for it to pass.

"Why did the dead have to be buried fifty miles from home?" I moaned, as we impatiently followed the cars.

It was after 3:00 when we got to Jean's house and met my tearful bride who thought she'd been jilted. Her mama was more nervous than the bride wondering how they'd ever live down the groom not showing up.

Jean looked angelic in her ankle-length white pique dress. She wore a small black and white hat with a white veil covering her hair. The white roses in her bouquet couldn't match her beautiful face when turned toward me as she walked down the aisle.

Jean's brother was a florist and filled the church with roses and carnations which flooded the church with perfume.

My little brother had saved his money and bought mud flaps for my car. When Jean and I walked out of the church, the first thing she saw were the chrome-lined mud flaps filled with red reflectors. "Wales," she whispered, "how could you?!"

"Hulon put them on. He was so proud, I couldn't hurt his feelings by taking them off. We will though. Don't worry," I assured her.

Forty years have now passed, and we have three fine children and five grandchildren. Jean has been my best supporter and constant companion, and by the time the Lord called me into full-time ministry, the Holy Spirit revealed to her she was not saved. She trusted Jesus as Lord and Savior, and her conversion filled us both with joy.

There was still one more person I prayed for daily. Mama. It took her a little longer than Jean to see that her good works would not get her to heaven.

34
Ain't That Something

✥

Walter lived only several months after I visited him in the hospital. A country preacher told me he went to see him before he died. The preacher said, "I asked if he was saved, and he told me 'Yes, sir! and you'd never believe it, but Wales Goebel led me to Jesus. Now ain't that something, of all people, Wales Goebel.'"

"Yes," I thought, as I remembered growing up in Tallapoosa, Georgia, "ain't that something." Joy welled up in my heart as I looked back and thought of all the Lord had done for me, through me, and in me.

One of my greatest griefs is going home where everybody remembers me like I was. When I try to be serious and tell them about the Lord, they want to remind me of some capers I pulled. I tell them that's all in the past.

"You mean if I offered you a drink of the best moonshine you ever tasted, you'd turn it down?" they ask.

"Sure would," I say, as serious as a judge.

"Boy! You sure have changed," they usually just shake their heads and walk away.

I remember Walter as the bratty little brother of my good buddy Curtis. There were several older brothers in the family, but Curtis and I were the same age. We fought as much as any two boys in town but never had a mad fight. I mean we didn't scratch each other like my brother and I did when we fought. Curtis and I just wrestled.

Curtis's mama and daddy had a shot house during the '30s. There were no jobs, and this was one way a man could feed his family. He must have done a good business because all their children wore nice clothes.

I used to tell Mama that Mrs. Carlton's floors were so clean you could eat off them. They weren't common wooden floors, but linoleum. She always invited me to come in and have a fresh tomato sandwich when I was playing at their house. They were the best sandwiches I ever ate, two big slices of tomato with several strips of bacon between soft white bread. Maybe we were a little hungrier back during the Depression.

I wondered why men, black and white, knocked at their back door. Curtis finally told me that the glass Mrs. Carlton handed the men was filled with moonshine, not water. She charged a quarter per glass and kept the money in a fruit jar hidden behind the flour sack on her kitchen shelf.

I told Mama about this marvelous money-making business and suggested she do the same. I didn't understand her answer then, "I may be poor, but I'm proud."

Walter was the youngest of all the Carlton kids and tagged along wherever Curtis and I went. No matter how many rocks we threw at him or what we threatened, he was always just behind us. We gave up trying to escape from him and just let him come along. Even when we went to the pool hall, little Walter was right with us. He was so small we stood him on a Coca-Cola box to watch us play. I had cut my younger brother out of my life, but we couldn't get rid of Walter.

When we all grew up, Curtis opened a nightclub with one of his brothers. Walter made it as a big-time gambler. He went to Nevada and won thousands of dollars but lost the same.

I lost contact with the Carlton boys over the years, but once when I was visiting in Tallapoosa, I went to see Mr. and Mrs. Carlton. I had heard they had given their lives to Christ. I don't know of anyone's salvation that surprised me more than theirs. If they were church people when I was growing up, I didn't know it.

I hardly got in their door before Mr. Carlton told me of his salvation experience. He was now driving a taxi and gave every person he drove a tract. God had done a wonderful work in both of their lives. I told them I'd like to see Curtis.

"I hope you can, and Wales, please talk to all our boys about Jesus," Mrs. Carlton said.

"I'll pray God will make a way so I can," I answered, as they walked to the front porch with me.

Years passed before my prayer was answered. Curtis called and told me Walter was in the hospital in Birmingham. He had cancer, and Curtis wanted me to go visit him.

"Sure I will, Curtis. I'm sorry to hear he's so sick," I said and prayed God would open Walter's heart when I told him about Jesus.

I walked down the hospital corridor and passed many doors of very sick people before I found Walter's room. Inwardly, I gasped when I saw little Walter in the bed as pale as the white sheet covering him. Curtis and another brother were there, too.

"How're you getting along, Walter?" I asked but knew the answer.

"You know, Wales, I made a lot of money gambling," he said, trying to avoid my question.

"I knew you were good at it, but now let's talk about Jesus." I knew he wasn't strong enough for small talk.

"I'd like to, Wales. I heard you got religion. I know I don't have long, and I need to get right with God."

Curtis and his brother started to leave, but I asked them to stay. "Your mama told me to tell each of you the good news of Jesus Christ." It wasn't the first time I had tried to fulfill Mrs. Carlton's request. Once when I was scheduled to speak at the First Baptist Church in Tallapoosa, I asked Mama to go over to Curtis's house and invite him to come to the service. She found the house and knocked on the door, but nobody came. Mama knew he was there, and since the front door was open, she hollered through the screen, "Curtis, come out here. I know you're in there."

Like a little boy, he came out. Mama said, "Wales wants you to come to church tonight and hear him preach. You need to hear what he has to say."

Polite as always, he said, "Yes, ma'am. But Mrs. Goebel, I don't need to listen to Wales. I grew up with him and know what kind of boy he was. Religious or not, he's still Wales."

But now Walter wasn't interested in what we used to do. He was dying and needed help. I told him how Jesus had saved me and changed me and that He would do the same for him, just as He had forgiven the thief on the cross.

"Walter, you give Him your life, and He will give you His," I said. "That doesn't seem to be a good deal for Jesus, but that's the way it is. He loves you so much, He'll take you just as you are."

Tears filled his eyes and ran down his thin pale face. "I'm ready," he said.

"All right then, you pray with me, 'Lord Jesus, take my life, forgive me my sins, save my soul, please come into my heart. Amen."

Like a little child he prayed word for word after me as I said the words slowly. I took my little pocket Bible out and opened it to Revelation 3:20. I read, "Behold, I stand at the door and knock, if anyone opens the door I will come in."

"Do you believe Jesus died for your sins and came into your heart when you asked, Walter?"

"Yes, I do," he said and wiped tears from his cheek with the sheet.

"Then let's pray again."

On his own, Walter prayed a nice prayer for a brand-new believer.

Turning to Curtis and his brother, I said, "You boys may not be given the same opportunity as Walter. Will you take Jesus right now as your Savior?"

They shook their heads, "No," but looked moved by what they had just witnessed. I patted Walter's hand and told him I'd see him in heaven and turned to leave. Curtis followed me and called, "Wales, wait a minute."

I waited as he walked toward me. "Wales, I believe in religion and respect it. There's a man who comes to my club on weekends and stands out front giving out tracts. I always give him a cold Coca-Cola. Whatcha think about that?"

"That's good, Curtis. That's a good deed, but it won't get you into heaven. You lack the one essential thing–Jesus."

I felt him tremble as he shook my hand. His eyes filled with tears as he thanked me for coming and helping Walter.

"Glad to," I told him. "You see, one day someone came to see me."

I just wish I could have helped all those boys I grew up with. Maybe I planted a seed for Curtis and his brother. God's Word doesn't come back void.

It's true. I was about as irreligious as the bootleggers and tavern-owners growing up. There were many storms in my life that brought me to Jesus. I didn't know at the time, but all of them would be used to bring me to the end of myself and make me into a man God could use.

35
Mama's Conversion

The telephone rang just as I walked in the back door at home. It was Mama. She didn't even say hello, just "You'd better sit down." Her voice was as excited as a little girl greeting her daddy.

"What's wrong?" I asked, but deep in my heart I knew what she was going to say. My good friend Elizabeth Newbold had visited Mama that day at my request.

"Nothing is wrong. For the first time, I can really say all is fine!"

In my spirit, I felt Mama was ready to receive the Lord, because she had turned mean toward me. She could be tough to other people, but not her boys. Lately, she was plain old grouchy.

"Whatcha want to tell me, Mama?" The volume of my voice brought Jean out of the kitchen. Her eyes lit up, for she had seen Elizabeth's car in Mama's driveway and knew Elizabeth was not only a great Bible teacher but could also lead a person to Christ.

Mama's joy came through the phone loud and clear, "I've been saved!"

That undid me. I was so emotional, I had to say, "Mama, let me call you right back." I wiped the tears from my eyes but couldn't contain the joy that flooded my heart.

I jumped up and hugged Jean. I felt like a weight had been lifted off me because my burden for Mama's conversion was gone. I had to sit down in my big chair beside the phone. Jean put her arms around me. She was crying, too. We prayed, thanking God for His goodness, kindness, and mercy that brought Mama to Himself.

Mama had moved to Birmingham and lived across the street from us. Just a phone conversation wouldn't do after praying for her for 16 years.

"Jean, I gotta go over there and see for myself. Want to come with me?"

"No, this is a special time for just the two of you. Go ahead," Jean said.

I walked across the street and gave Mama a bear hug. We both laughed and cried, for the sheer joy of the presence of Jesus was almost touchable. "Tell me about it, Mama," I said, as we sat on the porch glider.

"When Mrs. Newbold came to the door I knew why she was here. I said, 'You've come to save me.' She said, 'No, I can't save you. I came to tell you about Jesus who can forgive your sins and give you eternal life.' Wales, I don't know why it took so long for me to understand! I must have been blind."

"Mama, that's exactly what the Bible says. We are blind until God opens our eyes. It's wonderful that He made salvation so simple, but we can't understand with human reason. God loves us, but since we're sinners, we can't know His love until we realize Jesus died for our sins. Just knowing that fact doesn't make us Christian though. We must admit we need Him to wash away our sin and come into our hearts as our personal Savior. When we humble ourselves and ask Him to save us, He will."

We talked till the summer twilight faded and the stars came out. They were dim compared to the light in our eyes. I kept asking her over and over if she were to die now, did she know she would go to heaven.

"I sure do," she answered.

A June bug settled on a chair next to us. It crawled around inspecting the chair arm and then flew away.

"Did you see that, Mama?"

"I did," she answered.

"Do you remember me telling you when I was kicked out of college, I felt something had me by the leg the way Hulon had the string on a June bug?"

She nodded.

163

"Well, that bug just flew away. It wasn't tied down. It is free. That's what God has done for us both. We've been set free."

Mama thought for a minute before she answered, "Sure is good to be free."

"Yes, ma'am, it is."

Mama later asked me to get her a big-print Bible. She had the same hunger to know God's Word I had when I got saved. It's been over 20 years now since Mama was set free. She has grown in faith, knowledge, and love for the Lord and has even more love for her boys.

When I was young, I heard people say when their parents died, "I wish I had written to them more often or taken time to call." They felt guilty. I said to myself back then, "That will never happen to me and Mama."

In the last 25 years, I have arranged to take one day off during the week and spend it with Mama. Wednesday is the best time since I am away preaching on weekends. It is her day.

I call her around 10:00 and ask, "Guess who this is?"

"Am I getting a call from the President?"

"No, guess again."

"Why, it must be Billy Graham!"

"How did you know?" I say, and we both laugh.

"What time do you want to get out?"

"Anytime."

"Where do you want to go?"

She always says, "It doesn't matter as long as I am with you."

Jean and I pick her up about noon and our first stop is Wendy's. She enjoys their old-fashioned hamburgers. We don't go in, just order from the drive-through. The girls who work there recognize my voice and ask how Mama's doing.

"She's doing just fine. She's with me."

When we drive around to the pick-up window, Mama talks to them like they're her children. We pull out to the parking lot in front of Wal-Mart and sit and talk. Jean and I have coffee while Mama eats.

I ask what she'd like to do next, although I already know she loves to walk through one of the shopping malls. We visit all the stores that carry women's things. She insists I go in with her. By the middle of the afternoon, she has worn me out. I warn her not to get tired, and she lets me know she's not. She knows I'm the one who's tired.

"Well, I have had enough for one day. If you want, we can go home," Mama will reply.

We get into the car and I tell her it will be too late for her to prepare supper, so we'd better get a bite to eat.

"Can we go back to Wendy's?" she asks.

"Sure, if that's what you want," I say.

"Reckon I could have a chocolate milkshake with my hamburger?"

"Mama, whatever you want you can have."

"Well, I hate to spend your money. I know you don't have much."

"I've got just enough for an old-fashioned hamburger and a big ol' chocolate milkshake."

She smiles back at me.

We get home about dark. Jean and I go through her house, look under the beds and in all the closets to make sure no bugaboos are hiding.

Mama gives me a big hug and says, "This has been my very best Wednesday."

"Why, you told me that last week."

"Yes, but this was better."

"Mama, if you die tonight, where are you going?"

"You know," she replies.

"Yes, but tell me again." I never tire of hearing her answer.

"I'm going to heaven."

"How do you know?" I ask.

She used to tell me, "Because you saved me," and I would tell her, "No, I didn't save you. Who saved you?"

"Jesus died for all my sins, and He saved me," she says with conviction.

That answer, to this day, is the best music to my ears.

As Jean and I start to leave, Mama instructs me, "Don't let me see you coming out in the cold morning air for your paper without your sweater, sonny boy."

"Yes, ma'am."

"I mean it," she says.

"Yes, ma'am. I know you mean it," I reply, as serious as any little boy scolded by his mama.

I'll miss Mama when she dies. I often think about it, because she's not well. On several occasions, I've rushed her to the hospital. I dread the day when the doctor comes out and tells me, "I'm sorry. We couldn't help her."

Oh, sure it will hurt. But I will think, "Mama, you are like that ole' June bug now. At last you are truly free."

Probably not too many years after Mama goes to Heaven, I'll die, too. I wonder what it will be like to see her in her new heavenly body.

I can imagine her meeting me with smiles wreathing her face. Right off, she'll say, "Wales, guess what they have up here!"

"I don't know, Mama. I just got here."

She will reply, "They've got a shopping mall!"

We'll laugh, knowing I'll not get tired there. "Come on, Mama, for the next 10,000 years, just you and me."

And freer than the June bug, we'll walk arm in arm through the heavenly malls to Jesus' feet where there's never "a storm a-coming."

Post Script

✛

My ministry, which could include another 35 chapters, began when I received an invitation to speak in a local school. Schools have an unmistakable odor. I had forgotten that smell until I walked in one of the large high schools in Birmingham, Alabama, to meet Jackie. She was beautiful and beaming and full of a cheerleader's personality.

"Mr. Goebel, I am so excited about this meeting! I could hardly sleep last night." She was practically jumping up and down.

"You know, I couldn't sleep either, but not because I was 'so excited.' I was full of fear, all six feet, five inches and 230 pounds of me." I followed her down the hall, wondering why my car couldn't have had a flat tire, run out of gas, or had a wreck on the way. One place on earth I didn't want to be was at that high school or with that girl who was acting as if I were the greatest person ever to walk those hallowed halls.

Jackie introduced me to a teacher waiting in the large classroom where we were meeting. She said, "Mr. Goebel, I'm the club's sponsor. We are very grateful for you coming to speak to us. Jackie has been counting the days. This is a larger-than-usual group for our Bible club. Normally, we have only 10 to 15, but today there are over 100 here. Many are football players, and one is an assistant coach."

While more students came in and the sponsor made announcements, I sat next to Jackie and explained why I was their Bible club speaker. A few weeks previously, I had attended an organizational meeting of Youth for Christ. I had never met the other men who were present, but before the meeting was over, we were all fast friends. With the assistance of Youth for Christ, we agreed to start a ministry and have another meeting within the week to select a chairman and form a

167

board. We didn't need a treasurer because we started with zero money. Since we didn't have a YFC director, the board members would have to get the word out to the schools that this new ministry was starting in our city and county. How to do this was beyond me.

I continued to explain to Jackie that several weeks later our chairman called me. "Wales," he said, "I have just spoken to an excited Christian girl who attends Ensley High. She's a cheerleader and wants someone from YFC to come to her school and speak to their Bible club. Would you do it?"

"I don't know about that. What would I say? So far, the board hasn't done anything to report."

"Man alive! This is a great opportunity. Go tell them how Jesus saved you," he said.

"I could do that," I said. "So now, here I am sitting next to the 'excited Christian girl' who called."

Jackie said, "I'm so glad you're here. See that big guy sitting in the back row? He's going to be saved today."

I was shocked. "By me?"

"No, sir, by Jesus."

"Jackie, how much time do I have? Would 15 minutes be OK?"

"You'll have 35 minutes before the bell rings."

I was sure I couldn't talk that long, but to my amazement the whole time zipped by, and everyone was still seated and attentive. I asked if anyone would like to receive Christ as his Savior. Several indicated they would by raising their hand, and, lo and behold, the football player Jackie had pointed out was one of them.

I kept up with this fellow and was delighted when he received a scholarship to play for coach Paul Bryant. Through this young man's influence and testimony at the University of Alabama, many students were recruited to go to California to take evangelism training from Campus Crusade for Christ.

A few days later, the principal of Berry High School, with a student body of 2,000, called and asked me to speak. The school prided itself on strong discipline and was known for its high scholastic record and sports programs. Most of their graduates went on to college. I was very reluctant. I had never spoken to a large crowd. "I really don't think I can do it," I told the principal, trying to beg off.

"You should really consider doing this, Mr. Goebel," the principal said.

"Why do you say that?"

"In all the years I have been here, you are the first religious speaker our students have asked for."

"How many will there be?"

"We never know. Since it's a religious meeting, it is voluntary. The students usually come just to get out of class. You'll have several hundred."

At 9:00 AM on the appointed day, I waited in the principal's office, remembering the many times I sat in my principal's office during my high school days. This time I wasn't waiting to be paddled, but I was just as scared. I thought my heart would stop when the bell rang for the students to move into the gym. Why did I tell that Youth for Christ director I would help with the ministry? Why did I let our board chairman talk me into going to the first high school? They weren't paying me, so why not just get up and leave? But, I couldn't do that because out there somewhere were kids who had asked the principal to invite me.

I sat on the stage with the principal and watched more and more kids cram into the gym until there wasn't a seat left. A coach bounded up the steps and whispered something to the principal. I could tell it was some kind of emergency. "Good," I thought, "maybe the place is on fire, and I can go home. Or maybe it's a bomb scare. Maybe some parent has filed a law suit and the meeting can't go on." What else could it be?

The principal turned to me and said, "Mr. Goebel, we're overwhelmed by this response. We've never had to do this before, but we are going to have to move out to the football stadium."

I stood on the football field and looked up at the stands filled with a sea of young faces. I watched those on the back row as well as those sitting up front. For a moment, I imagined myself out there hearing for the first time a message on love that would take away all my hurts. If only someone had done the same for me back in high school, maybe I would have avoided a lot of storms that nearly blew me away. What if they had said, "Kids, God loves you and all He ever asks of you and me is that we, in turn, love Him?" My heart went out to them and I preached, actually preached, the love of God as found in Jesus' death and resurrection.

Over 600 came forward when I invited those who wished to accept Jesus as their Savior and Lord to come down front.

God was about to redirect my life.

Jean and I had a clear knowledge of God's call to work with young people. I was 36 years old. We left a successful residential construction business, and with our three small sons, moved out of a beautiful, two-story home in one of the finer subdivisions in Birmingham, into a small, cramped apartment.

We incorporated the Wales Goebel Ministry in 1967. Without Bible college or seminary training, we began a ministry that has proven to be truly a work of God. I began speaking to high school and college students across the Southeast. Soon, fraternities and sororities, college and high-school football, baseball and basketball coaches and teams were inviting me to share with them the Good News of what Christ had done in my life. God began to open church revivals and crusades, too.

In 1971, the ministry purchased three acres of property that had a small home on it. We added on to the house to make it into an office building, which has increased in size three times. The ministry staff began to grow, and there are now ten full-time members plus hundreds of volunteers.

Over the next 26 years, my staff and I have seen thousands of people come to a saving faith in Jesus Christ through revivals, conferences, counseling, and working with girls involved in crisis pregnancies.

In 1980, after counseling with many young girls who had experienced the trauma of abortion, I founded an organization called

Post Script

Sav-A-Life, Inc. By January of 1995, there were 41 affiliates in five southeastern states. These Sav-A-Life affiliates minister to over 40,000 girls a year.

The young mothers began asking that their babies be placed for adoption in Christian homes. An adoption agency was desperately needed. In 1981, I founded Lifeline Children's Services, Inc., and it has placed nearly 500 babies into homes of Christian parents.

God's next assignment was for us to build a home to house girls awaiting the birth of their babies. Forty acres of property was purchased, and our first home for unwed mothers was opened. In 1992, a second home was built. Over 700 girls have been cared for in these homes. A third home is being planned.

Through the burden of Mrs. Ruth Wooten, a missionary with Sav-A-life, Inc., the ministry of Sex and Family Education (SAFE) was started. Today it reaches thousands of young people across America and in foreign countries.

This could not have happened without God's blessing. He gave me a heavy burden for lost and hurting souls, especially young people.

Ezekiel 22:30 tells how God is seeking a man who will "build up the wall and stand in the gap before Me for the land, that I should not destroy it." God called me. My gap is young people, and I have not been disobedient to His calling.

As Dr. Bill Bright, founder of Campus Crusade for Christ, has stated, "Surely the hand of God is upon the ministry of Wales Goebel."